THE STRANGE DEATH
OF
LORD CASTLEREAGH

ICON

H. MONTGOMERY HYDE

THE STRANGE DEATH
OF
LORD CASTLEREAGH

ICON BOOKS LIMITED

PRINTING HISTORY

First published by William Heinemann Ltd in 1959

© by H. Montgomery Hyde 1959

Published as an Icon Book in 1967

Cover design by Raymond E. Meylan, M.S.I.A.

Icon Books are published by Icon Books Ltd.,
9 Down Street, Mayfair, W.1, and are printed
in Great Britain by Hunt Barnard & Co., Ltd.,
Aylesbury, Buckinghamshire.

FOR
ALISTAIR

'There is some mystery about this which perhaps Time will explain; but whatever it was, it must have been something very serious to have led to such an act.'

Baron Neumann, Counsellor at the Austrian Embassy in London, on Castlereagh's death, 12th August 1822. THE DIARY OF PHILIP VON NEUMANN (edited by E. B. Chancellor), Vol. 1, p. 100.

CONTENTS

Preface

My interest in the subject of these pages was first aroused by a chance visit to Mount Stewart, Lord Castlereagh's family home in County Down, more than thirty years ago. It inspired me to write an account of his early career in Ireland, which was published under the title of THE RISE OF CASTLEREAGH in 1933.

In the course of my researches among the Castlereagh Papers, now preserved at Mount Stewart, it was inevitable that I should come across references to the statesman's sudden and unexpected death by his own hand in 1822 and its attendant circumstances, which have long been veiled in mystery. This aspect was outside the scope of my original work. But for some time I have felt that all the known facts surrounding the tragedy of Castlereagh's suicide should be placed on record, since in this respect his reputation in private has suffered as much from whispered calumny as his public record from open attacks. Important and hitherto unknown details of his private life have recently been revealed by the letters and diaries of Princess Lieven and Mrs Arbuthnot. These include an interesting unpublished biographical sketch of Castlereagh by Princess Lieven, the original manuscript of which is in my own collection. I have made use of this and other material to give the most feasible explanation of the mystery that I have been able to find. I believe it to be the true one.

For access to documents and other material in their possession I wish to express my particular thanks to Edith Marchioness Dowager of Londonderry, D.B.E., the Marquess of Londonderry and the Duke of Wellington. To

Messrs. John Murray, publishers of *The Private Letters of Princess Lieven to Prince Metternich*, edited by Peter Quennell, and to Macmillan & Co. Ltd., publishers of *The Journal of Harriet Arbuthnot*, edited by the Duke of Wellington and Francis Bamford, I am indebted for permission to quote from these editions.

H. M. H.

CHAPTER ONE

Inquest and Funeral

I

TOWARDS MIDDAY ON MONDAY, 12th August, 1822, rumours began to circulate in London that the Marquess of Londonderry, Foreign Secretary and Leader of the House of Commons, who to all outward appearances was in the best of health a few days previously, had suddenly died.

Sixteen months earlier Lord Londonderry had succeeded his father in the peerage, which, being an Irish one, entitled him to continue to sit in the Lower House of Parliament. For many years before that event, he had been known by his courtesy title of Viscount Castlereagh, and indeed it is by that title that contemporaries and historians alike remember him. A comparatively young man—he was only fifty-three at this time—Robert Stewart, Viscount Castlereagh and second Marquess of Londonderry, had spent most of his life in the public service as a staunch Tory and disciple of Mr. Pitt. He had held a number of important political offices, and somehow these posts assumed a particular importance during the period in which he filled them. He was Chief Secretary for Ireland at the time of the Rebellion of 1798 and the subsequent Act of Union, which joined that distressful country with the rest of the United Kingdom; he was at the War Office during the Peninsular War and was instrumental in giving the Duke of Wellington his first military command in Spain; he became Foreign Minister in 1812 in the closing stages of the struggle with Napoleon;

he had played an active part in the negotiations for a European settlement, which took place in Vienna and Paris in 1814 and 1815, and he continued to represent his country at the various conferences of Foreign Ministers, which were summoned to other Continental meeting-places in the years immediately following the general peace settlement. He had led the House of Commons for the past ten years and, since the titular Prime Minister, the Earl of Liverpool, was in the House of Lords and had latterly become unpopular with King George IV, Castlereagh was also Prime Minister in all but name. It seemed only a matter of time before he succeeded his chief as the nominal as well as the real head of the Government.

Castlereagh's last public appearance had been at the prorogation of Parliament, a ceremony which was performed by His Majesty in person less than a week previously. The session had been a particularly arduous one, and although Castlereagh in chatting with several fellow members at the Bar of the Upper House remarked that he was glad it had come to an end, to the casual observer he appeared in his usual vigorous health and good spirits. A colleague's wife, Mrs. Arbuthnot, on whom he had called on his way to the House, noted in her diary for that day how handsome he looked in his dress-clothes. 'It does me good to see him,' she added. He was known to be about to set out with his wife for the Continent to attend another Foreign Ministers' conference, and a steam packet had already been engaged to convey him and his staff to Calais. The last meeting of the Cabinet, at which he had been present, had taken place a few days previously and had been for the purpose of obtaining approval of the instructions which he had drafted for his own use at the conference. In these circumstances many people could hardly believe the news that the Minister was dead when they first heard it. But the rumours persisted and their effect was immediately felt on the Stock Exchange, where Consols fell by a half per cent soon after one o'clock.

In the afternoon a King's Messenger was seen to drive up to the Foreign Office in a post-chaise and four. He had come from Cray Farm, the Minister's country place at North Cray in Kent and he brought with him official confirmation of the sad news. But newspaper reporters could discover no details. The servants at Lord Castlereagh's town house in St. James's Square refused to say anything further beyond confirming that their master had died. It was known that he suffered from gout and consequently the two London evening newspapers, *The Traveller* and *The Courier*, came out with the story that this complaint had 'suddenly attacked the stomach and terminated his life'. The morning papers for next day went to press with a similar story, but one of them was able to appear with a 'stop press' report which it had received at a late hour 'from a quarter we can depend on' and which showed that His Lordship's death was not the result of 'gout in the stomach' but of something infinitely more distressing. It now appeared that the Foreign Minister, in a fit of mental depression, had committed suicide by severing the carotid artery in his neck. In doing so he had fallen into his doctor's arms and, in the picturesque language of *The Morning Herald*, 'was a corpse in a moment'.

Castlereagh was the third Member of Parliament within the last few years to die by his own hand, and in the welter of speculation which the news produced it was natural that the cases of the other two suicides, Whitbread and Romilly, should have been recalled. 'Mr. Whitbread, Sir Samuel Romilly and the Marquess of Londonderry,' wrote *The Traveller* in a leading article on 13th August, 'three public men who have, within not many years, died in the same way, were men who, though differing in other qualities, were remarkable for firmness of mind and purpose.' The article went on to state that it was at first determined to keep

13

the cause of the Minister's death secret, but that this was, if practicable, an unworthy determination. 'Whatever Lord Londonderry's merits or demerits may have been,' the article continued, 'there is enough of good sense in the people not to allow the manner of his death in any way to affect the estimate of his character and intentions. It is idle to talk of Lord Londonderry as a great man, and it is just as idle to talk of him as a very vulgar and ordinary one. A man, who so long, and with a degree of credit among his own party, held power against enemies and rivals, must either have had some striking qualities, or that host of smaller virtues, which as Bacon well imagines it, "make up fortune". It is a sort of tribute to his memory that his character becomes a matter of examination and censure.'

There were not lacking numerous critics ready to participate in such an exercise. They comprised for the most part members of the Whig Opposition in Parliament and their supporters in the country, besides many Irish patriots who regarded 'bloody Castlereagh' as the betrayer of his native Ireland. The poet, Lord Byron, voiced the patriotic feeling in doggerel verse:

So *He* has cut his throat at last!—He? Who?
The man who cut his country's long ago.

The popular Whig view was expressed by the gossiping back-bench M.P. Thomas Creevey, in a letter to his niece. 'Death settles a fellow's reputation in no time,' wrote Mr. Creevey, 'and now that Castlereagh is dead, I defy any human being to discover a single feature of his character that can stand a moment's criticism. By experience, good manners and great courage, he managed a corrupt House of Commons pretty well, with some address. This is the whole of his intellectual merit. He had a limited understanding and no knowledge, and his whole life was spent in an avowed, cold-blooded contempt of every honest public principle. A worse, or, if he had had talent and ambition for it, a more dangerous public man never existed.'

A more considered Whig view was recorded by the diarist, Charles Greville, writing on the day after the event:

As a Minister he is a great loss to his party, and still greater to his friends and Dependents, to whom he was the best of Patrons; to the Country I think he is none. Nobody can deny that his talents were great, and perhaps he owed his influence and authority as much to his character as to his abilities. His appearance was dignified and imposing; he was affable in his manner and agreeable in society. The great feature was a cool and determined courage, which gave an appearance of resolution and confidence to all his actions, inspired his friends with admiration and excessive devotion to him and caused him to be respected by his most violent opponents.

As a speaker he was prolix, monotonous, and never eloquent, except, perhaps, for a few minutes when provoked into a passion by something which had fallen in debate. But, notwithstanding these defects, and still more the ridicule which his extraordinary phraseology had drawn upon him, he was always heard with attention. He never spoke ill; his speeches were continually replete with good sense and strong argument, and though they seldom offered much to admire, they generally contained a great deal to be answered. I believe he was considered one of the best Managers of the H[ouse] of Commons who ever sat in it, and he was eminently possessed of good taste, good humour and agreeable manners which are more requisite to make a good Leader than eloquence, however brilliant.

With these qualities it may be asked why he was not a better Minister, and who can answer that question? or can ever say that he did not pursue a policy which he conscientiously believed to be most advantageous to his country? Nay, more, who can say but from surmise and speculation that it was not the best?

I believe that he was seduced by his vanity, that his head was turned by emperors, kings, and congresses, and that he was resolved that the country he represented should play as conspicuous part as any other in the political Dramas that were enacted on the Continent. The result of his policy is this, that we are mixed up in the affairs of the Continent in a manner we have never been before, and which entails upon as endless negotiations and enormous expenses.

The most generous tribute, and no doubt the truest paid by a political opponent, came from Henry Brougham, Whig Radical lawyer, who from his place on the Opposition Front Bench had faced the late Foreign Minister and his Cabinet colleagues across the Table of the House of Commons for the past decade and had been in frequent conflict with him. 'Well! This is a considerable event in point of size,' wrote Brougham, when he heard the news. 'Put all their men together in one scale, and poor Castlereagh in the other— single he plainly weighed them down . . . one can't help feeling a little for him, after being pitted against him for several years pretty regularly. It is like losing a connection. Also, he was a *gentleman*. And the only one amongst them.'

2

While messengers were being sent off to inform the King, who was in Scotland, and the various members of the Government who were also out of town, of what had happened to the Foreign Secretary, Mr. Joseph Carter, the Coroner for West Kent, arrived at Cray Farm to conduct an inquest on the body of the dead nobleman, as he was bound by law to do. Shortly before three o'clock in the afternoon of 13th August, the Coroner and thirteen gentlemen from the neighbourhood who composed the jury assembled in the drawing-room of the house. They sat round a large table with the Coroner at their head, while the servants of the establishment ranged themselves round the lower end, several weeping profusely, since the late Marquess had been a well-loved master. No attempt was made to keep the occasion secret, and anyone who appeared at the gates of the house was admitted. It is to this fact that we owe the detailed account which was subsequently published in the newspapers at the time.

"Gentlemen of the jury," said the Coroner, "you have been summoned and sworn to inquire into the causes of death of a nobleman, who stood perhaps as high in the public estimation as any man in the country. That his lordship has met his death under particular circumstances you doubtless must have learned. But it is my duty to inform you, gentlemen, that you must remove from your minds all impressions which are not borne out by the evidence." Having started thus correctly, the Coroner went on practically to direct the jury as to the verdict they should bring in and which he trusted would be that which all good men desired. "If the facts which I have heard are proved in evidence," he observed, "I think no man can doubt that at the time he committed the rash act his lordship was labouring under a mental delusion. If, however, it should unfortunately appear that there is not sufficient evidence to prove what are generally considered the indications of a disordered mind, I trust, gentlemen, that you will pay some attention to my humble opinion, which is that no man could be in his proper senses at the moment he committed so rash an act as self-murder." The Coroner concluded his opening remarks by expressing his pleasure at seeing so respectable a body of gentlemen and adding the hope that they would acquit themselves of their important duty to the satisfaction of the public, as well as of their own consciences.

The object of this advice was to prevent the jury from bringing in a verdict of deliberate suicide, or *felo de se*. This would have meant that, instead of being interred with all possible pomp and ceremony in Westminster Abbey, as his widow hoped, Castlereagh's remains would be liable, under an ancient law, to be buried at a cross-roads, with a stake driven through his body.

The jury's first duty was to view the corpse, which was lying upstairs on the blood-stained floor of the dressing-room where it had originally fallen. Since this chamber was separated by only a thin partition from the adjacent bedroom where the widowed Lady Londonderry was still prostrated by grief, the members of the jury were asked to remove their shoes before entering the dressing-room so as not to disturb the Marchioness. This they accordingly did and filed upstairs into the death-chamber in silence. All that remained of Castlereagh was lying face downwards and with the feet towards the window. He was wearing a dressing-gown and a handkerchief was tied round his head. The jury inspected the small wound on the side of the neck, and then returned to the drawing-room without a word being spoken.

The first witness to be called was Lady Londonderry's maid, Mrs. Anne Robinson. She was examined by the Coroner and began her evidence by saying that her master had been unwell for the past fortnight. Two nights previously, that is, on the night of Sunday 11th August, he rang the bell in his bedroom. "At least I suppose it was he." She answered it, and he asked why Lady Londonderry had not been to see him. Mrs. Robinson told him that his wife had been with him all day.

"Had her ladyship, in point of fact, been with him?" the Coroner asked this witness.

"She had," the maid replied, "and was then in the adjoining room."

"Did you again enter the room?"

"I did. He rang the bell again and asked me if Dr. Bankhead had been to see him."

Dr. Bankhead was Castlereagh's personal physician and had been staying in the house since the previous evening.

"I said he had and had been with him a great part of the preceding night," the witness continued. "He then asked me if he had talked any nonsense to Dr. Bankhead. My reply was that I did not remain in the room during the conversation."

"Was this the fact?"

"It was."

"Did you then leave the room?"

"I did."

"What happened afterwards?"

"He rang the bell of his bedroom again, at seven o'clock on Monday morning, that is, yesterday morning. I answered it. When I went into the room he asked me what I wanted there. I made no reply, but her ladyship said, 'Anne, his lordship wants his breakfast.' Her ladyship was then in bed. I left the room and brought the breakfast. He found fault with the breakfast and said it was not a breakfast fit for him. He said there was no butter there. The butter, however, was on the tray and the breakfast was such as he usually had."

"Was there anything in his manner on this occasion, which appeared to you extraordinary?"

"Yes. It struck me as uncommon. His voice was sharp and severe, which was very unusual with him."

"Were you again summoned to the apartment?"

"I was. About half-past seven the bell rang again. I answered it and, on entering, his lordship asked me if Dr. Bankhead had come down from town yet. I answered him that Dr. Bankhead had slept in the house. He said he wished to see him. I went to the doctor and told him my lord wished to see him. When my lord desired me to call Dr. Bankhead, my lady was in the room, and she followed me to the door to speak to me. My lord, on seeing us together, said there was a conspiracy against him. After I had told Dr. Bankhead of my lord's wish, I returned to the room and told my lord that he would be with him in two minutes. As soon as my lady was ready to go into her dressing-room, and had shut the door, I went back to the door by which I had entered. My lord was then sitting up in bed. As soon as my lady had retired, my lord got out of bed, and shortly after opened the bedroom door and rushed by me towards his own dressing-room."

The witness was then asked several questions about the precise situation of the different upstairs rooms. She explained that the common sleeping room, which the late Marquess shared with his wife, opened into a passage, on either side of which was a dressing-room, Lady Londonderry's on the left and his lordship's on the right. At the end of the passage was another door, leading to Dr. Bankhead's room.

"I called to Dr. Bankhead and said my lord wanted him," the maid continued. "Dr. Bankhead immediately came up and followed my lord into his dressing-room. Immediately on his entrance, I heard him exclaim, 'My lord!' or 'My God!' I went directly into the room and saw my lord in Dr. Bankhead's arms. I remained in the room till he laid my lord on the floor, with his face to the ground."

Mrs. Robinson went on to say that she saw blood running from her master's body while the doctor held him; she also saw a knife in his hand. She then identified a small penknife with a blade about two inches in length and nearly half an inch in width, crooked towards the end, as the knife in question.

"Did you see the deceased use the knife, or see the wound, in the bedroom?"

"No. I did not."

"Did you perceive any wound or blood, while he was in the bedroom?"

"No. I did not."

"Are you quite sure there was no blood upon him while he was in his bedroom?"

"Quite sure."

"Are you quite sure no person went into the bedroom during the interval of which you have spoken, but Dr. Bankhead?"

"I am quite sure that no person did."

Turning to the jury, the Coroner explained that the purpose of these questions was to show that the act must have been done by the deceased himself and not by any other individual.

The remainder of this witness's examination was concerned with her knowledge of the late Marquess's mental condition at the time of his death and shortly before. This, Mrs. Robinson declared, was 'very bad', 'very incorrect', and 'very wild in everything he said and did'.

"Can you give us any particular words or expressions which he used from whence we may be able to judge of the state of his mind?"

"I can say, in the first place, that he asked me for a box which he said Lord Clanwilliam had given to me, when Lord Clanwilliam never gave me any box.* And he wished me to give him his keys, although they were in his own possession and he had them about him."

"Did he express any apprehensions of the persons about him?"

*Richard, 3rd Earl of Clanwilliam (1795-1879), was Parliamentary Under-Secretary of State for Foreign Affairs at this time.

"Yes. During the last fortnight he repeatedly said some persons had conspired against him."

"What other observation did you make on his general conduct?"

"He was very wild, and particularly on the last day before his death."

"In his manner?"

"Yes. In his manner. He was very severe."

"In speaking?"

"Yes."

"What was his general manner?"

"Always mild and kind. Very much so."

"Had he expressed any particular apprehensions about this conspiracy? What words did he use?"

"When he saw two people speaking together, my lady and Dr. Bankhead, he always said, 'There is a conspiracy laid against me.'"

"I would ask you whether, during Sunday and the preceding days, there was anything in his manner which induced you to think he was not in his right mind?"

"Yes, many."

"State some of them."

"He scolded my lady on Sunday afternoon, because, so he said, she had not been with him all day and had entirely forsaken him, although she had been with him all the morning. This was in the afternoon."

The Coroner's last question to Mrs. Robinson was calculated to have the effect on the jury which he plainly desired.

"You have no doubt that his mind was disordered for some time prior to his death?"

"Not the least. That is my firm persuasion, confirmed by all I observed."

The next witness to be called at the inquest was the dead man's physician, Dr. Charles Bankhead. The son of a Presbyterian minister from the north of Ireland, Dr. Bankhead had known Castlereagh almost since the time of his first election to the old Irish Parliament in Dublin in 1790, and he had known the other members of the Londonderry family, whom he had also attended professionally.

Dr. Bankhead stated that he lived in Lower Brook Street and was a Doctor of Physic. About five o'clock on the previous Friday afternoon, 9th August, he had received a note from Lady Londonderry begging him to come as soon as he could to see her husband at their house in St. James's Square. Her note stated that she was very anxious about his lordship, as she thought he was very ill and very nervous, that they were to leave town for North Cray at seven o'clock the same evening and that she hoped he would come before that hour.

"I arrived in St. James's Square about six o'clock," said the doctor, "and found Lord and Lady Londonderry alone in the drawing-room. On feeling his lordship's pulse, I perceived that he was exceedingly ill. He complained of a severe headache and confusion of recollection. He looked pale and very much distressed in manner. I said I thought it necessary that he should be cupped, and that in the meantime I would stay and dine with Lady Londonderry and himself till the cupper came. The cupper soon arrived and took seven ounces of blood from the nape of his lordship's neck. After the operation was performed he seemed to express himself very much relieved, and I advised him to lay himself quietly down on the sofa for half an hour and, as he had scarcely eaten any dinner, to take a dish of tea before he got into his carriage to go to North Cray. He did as I advised. He lay down for half an hour and drank two dishes of tea."

The doctor declared that he waited until Lady Londonderry and his lordship got into their carriage in order to go down to North Cray. "At his departure he said to me that, as I must be sure he was very, very ill, he would expect me to come to North Cray on Saturday night and stay that night and if possible all Sunday—to which I assented." Dr. Bankhead added that he gave him some aperient medicine to be taken on Saturday morning, so that he might know the effect of it when he arrived at night. The doctor stated that he knew his patient took these powders on Saturday and that he had remained in bed all that day until he arrived. (This latter piece of information having been obtained from someone in the house, the Coroner stated that it was inadmissible as hearsay evidence.)

Dr. Bankhead went on to say that he arrived at Cray on Saturday afternoon and immediately went up to his lordship's bedroom, as he understood his patient had not been up all day. "On entering his bedroom," said the doctor, "I thought his manner of looking at me particularly suspicious and alarming. He said it was very odd that I should come into his bedroom first before going into the dining-room below. I answered that I had dined in town and knowing that the family were at dinner downstairs I had come to visit him."

Upon this, according to the witness, Castlereagh made a remark which surprised his doctor exceedingly. It was to the effect that the doctor seemed particularly grave in his manner and that something must be amiss. He then asked the doctor abruptly whether he had anything unpleasant to tell him. "I answered no," said Bankhead, "and that I was surprised at his question and the manner in which it was put." Castlereagh then said that he 'had reason to be suspicious in some degree', but that he hoped that his doctor would be 'the last person who would engage in anything that would be injurious to him'. His manner of saying this was so unusual and so disturbed as to satisfy Dr. Bankhead that his patient was 'at the moment labouring under a mental delusion'. After begging him to keep quiet, the doctor prescribed some more cooling and aperient medicine, and put him on a diet of slops only.

"I remained with him for a great part of Saturday night and till perhaps nearly one o'clock on Sunday morning," Dr. Bankhead went on. "Though his fever was not high at any part of the time, yet the incoherence of his speech and the uncomfortableness of his manner continued. He remained so through Sunday. I was with him until half-past twelve o'clock on Sunday night. I advised him to be as tranquil as possible, to ask Lady Londonderry to come to bed and to endeavour to get some sleep. I remained at Cray all night and slept in a room very near theirs and opening into the same passage."

On the following morning about seven o'clock, according to Bankhead, Mrs. Robinson, Lady Londonderry's maid, came to his bedroom door and asked if he was dressed as his lordship wished to see him 'by and by'. The doctor answered that he was ready to come at that moment, but Mrs. Robinson replied, 'No, he does not wish to see you yet a little as her ladyship has not left the bedroom.' In about half an hour Mrs. Robinson returned and said that his lordship would be glad to see him immediately, as her ladyship was putting on her gown to go into the dressing-room. Dr. Bankhead thereupon followed the maid along the passage to the door of the main bedroom, which was open. He could see that Castlereagh was not there. The maid then said to him, 'My lord is just gone into his own dressing-room.'

Dr. Bankhead immediately stepped into the dressing-room, which was a long narrow apartment with a window at the end opposite the door. Castlereagh was standing in his dressing-gown with his front towards the window, but with his face towards the ceiling, as if he were looking at the ceiling. The moment he heard the doctor's step, and without turning round, he exclaimed, 'Bankhead, let me fall upon your arm. 'Tis all over!' The doctor moved towards him as quickly as possible, thinking he was fainting and going to fall.

"Did he see you?" asked the Coroner.

"No. I was running into the room. He felt himself dropping. I ran upon him and caught him in my arms."

"Did he appear to be falling?"

"Yes, he was falling. As he fell on me, I saw that he had a knife in his right hand, very firmly clenched."

"Did you see him use it?"

"No."

"Are the jury to understand that he used it before you saw him?"

"Certainly," replied the witness. "For as I caught him, I saw the knife bloody, and in falling a burst of blood took place like a torrent from a watering-pot. I was unable to support him, and he fell on the floor."

"Could the wound be inflicted while you were coming from the door?"

"I think it was done the instant I put my foot on the threshold of the door. From the nature of the wound, death must have followed in the twinkling of an eye. There could not be less than three quarts of blood which flowed from him in one minute. I am quite satisfied that it was not a minute from my entering the room till he was dead. His death was almost instantaneous. He never uttered another word."

"You are quite sure," queried the Coroner, "from all you saw and heard and from your own good sense that he used the knife himself?"

"It is impossible that it could have been done by any other human being," answered Dr. Bankhead. "There was no one in the room with him but myself, and death must necessarily follow in half a minute from the infliction of such a wound."

The Coroner then informed the jury that, the act being once proved, it was necessary to inquire into the state of his lordship's mind at the time he committed it.

"I have not the least hesitation in saying, from knowing the deceased intimately for the past thirty years," Dr. Bankhead declared, "that he was perfectly insane."

"From what period?" asked the Coroner.

"I had noticed a great decline in him for some weeks, in his general habit and in his health, but I was not aware of the mental delusion under which he was labouring, till within three or four days of his decease."

This concluded Dr. Bankhead's evidence. There were a number of other witnesses waiting to be examined, and some discussion now took place in private between the Coroner and the jury as to which of them should be heard. Eventually the foreman of the jury intimated that they had listened to enough evidence to enable them to return a verdict. After retiring for a short time, they recorded the following, embodied in a document, which seemed to have been prepared in advance for them on legal advice, which they all signed.

That on an inquest taken at the house of the late most noble Robert, Marquis of Londonderry, at North Cray, in the county of Kent, on Tuesday the 13th August, on view of the body of the said Marquis, we, the jurors, on our oaths, say that the said Marquis of Londonderry, on the 12th of August, and for some time previously, under a grievous disease of mind, did labour and languish, and by reason of the said disease, became delirious and not of sound mind; and that on the said 12th of August, in the said parish, while labouring under such disease, did, with a certain knife of iron or steel, upon himself make an assault and did strike and cut and stab himself on the carotid artery; and gave himself one mortal wound of the length of one inch and of the depth of two inches; of which said wound he did then and there instantly die; and being under a state of mental delusion in manner aforesaid, and by the means aforesaid, did kill and destroy himself, and did not come by his death through the means of any other person or persons whatsoever.

Before dismissing the jury, the Coroner had a few more words to say to them, which were allowed to be taken down by the Press.

"That which I have to offer will, I think, tend to make these proceedings as satisfactory to the world as I think they must be to your own conscience," he said to the jurors in endorsing their verdict. "A great number of witnesses could be brought forward to prove that the mind of the deceased has been afflicted for a longer period than has been supposed or than appears from the evidence submitted to you this day. They would carry back the commencement of that derangement under which he laboured to a period anterior to Friday last. I state this, as his appearance among his colleagues on that day—I believe before the King-in-Council—might cause a conflict in some minds and induce a suspicion that the fatal act was not committed under the influence of insanity. The witnesses, however, who could have proved what I have mentioned, it was not thought necessary to examine. I shall, however, read a letter to you from a very high and distinguished character which can, and if necessary will, be verified. It is from the Duke of Wellington, and though it cannot now be received as evidence, nor could it have been before your verdict was returned, its contents will be satisfactory to you, as it will show what was his Grace's opinion of Lord Londonderry's mind on the 9th of August."

The letter, which was addressed to Dr. Bankhead, was in the following terms:

London, Aug. 9, 1822

Dear Sir,

I called upon you with the intention of talking to you about Lord Londonderry, and of requesting you would call upon him. He promised me that he would send for you, but lest he should not, I entreat you to find some pretence of going down to him.

I entertain no doubt he is very unwell. It appears that he has been overworked during the session, and that his mind is overpowered for the moment and labours under a delusion. I state the impression made upon me in the interview I have just had with him. I told him that this was my impression, and I think it is his own, and he will probably communicate it to you. But, lest he should not, I tell you what I think, begging you will never mention to anybody what I have told you.

I am setting out this moment for the Netherlands. I would have stayed with Lord Londonderry, but he would not allow me. I shall be very much obliged to you, if you will write me a line, and have it left at my house, to let me know how you find him, and particularly if you think I am mistaken.

Ever, dear Sir,
Yours most faithfully,
WELLINGTON

Dr. Charles Bankhead, M.D.

To this letter the Duke had added a postscript: 'I believe he is going down to Cray this afternoon.'

Although they had been married for nearly thirty years and were to all appearances and in fact an ideally devoted couple, Castlereagh and his wife had no children. His nearest male relative was his younger half-brother Charles, Lord Stewart, at that time British Ambassador to Austria, who now succeeded to his titles and Irish property. It was impossible, of course, in the slow travelling conditions of those days, for word to reach Stewart in Vienna in time to enable him to return to England for the funeral. Thus he had to be represented by his son Frederick, the new Lord Castlereagh, a youth of seventeen, who was already in England and arrived at Cray immediately he heard the fatal news. At first the widowed Lady Londonderry would talk to no one except her sister, Lady Suffield, who happened to be staying in the house at the time. But when Lord Clanwilliam, the Parliamentary Under-Secretary for Foreign Affairs and their particular friend and neighbour in County Down, appeared in the house, she consented to receive him. As Clanwilliam entered her bedroom and took her by the hand, she burst into a flood of tears and said, 'You I wished to see, for he loved you dearly.' She also wished Clanwilliam to take charge of the funeral arrangements and inform the various friends and relatives, who should be written to. She spoke to him of her wish that her husband should be buried in Westminster Abbey, instead of at Cray or in the family burying place in the north of Ireland. Clanwilliam promised to see the Prime Minister, Lord Liverpool, on the subject as soon as possible after the inquest. 'I certainly think it were most desirable,' Clanwilliam wrote to Stewart the same day, 'and that the funeral should be publick and that a fitting monument should be raised over the remains of him, to whom his friends were devoted and whom his country will honour to the latest posterity.'

Lord Liverpool was quite agreeable to the suggestion of an Abbey funeral, and immediately wrote to the Dean of Westminster, who gave the necessary directions. The ceremony was accordingly fixed to take place from St. James's Square on the following Tuesday, 20th August, at nine o'clock in the morning. Lord Stewart was informed of the details by his brother-in-law, Sir Henry Hardinge. 'Upon these arrangements I can only express the most unqualified approbation,' wrote Hardinge. 'His remains deserve to repose in the most honoured sanctuary and are to be placed quite close to those of his great friend and predecessor, Mr. Pitt. Any other arrangement would have been as unfeeling as unjust, and I know your heart and its unbounded love for him too well not to be certain that you will receive consolation in the reflexion that his burial will be as honourable and public as his life. It is true the line has been drawn only to invite by letter his relatives and personal friends from a sense of delicacy, that his family did not think it becoming to solicit or canvass for attendance, but many members of both Houses are of their own accord coming up to Town and joining the procession in the Abbey. The *corps diplomatique* have requested to attend, many military and naval officers, and all his tradesmen, with several neighbours both high and low from Cray. There never was since his death more unfeigned demonstration of love and sympathy from all classes of persons.'

Meanwhile the undertaker and his men had arrived at Cray Farm from London and, after the body was washed and laid out, it was placed in a plain wooden coffin, which was encased in lead. The coffin was taken to the room which Castlereagh used as a study, and it remained there until the evening before the funeral. About half-past nine on that evening, the coffin was carried out to a hearse which stood

31

waiting outside the front door; this vehicle was covered with sable plumes and drawn by six horses. The procession then moved off, headed by the undertaker Mr. Newton of Wardour Street and his two assistants on horseback. The hearse was followed by a mourning coach, containing the dead man's land agent, house steward, cook and valet. Two grooms brought up the rear, also on horseback. As the procession passed at a walking pace through North Cray, the villagers turned out to pay their last respects, and the bell of the parish church tolled a requiem. Later the procession broke into a sharp trot for two or three miles, but afterwards it slackened pace, especially when passing through different villages, including Deptford and Eltham. At New Cross turnpike the cortège left the Kent Road, taking the direction of Kennington. Their route lay past Camberwell Green. There a Fair happened to be in progress, and the merriments occasioned by this spectacle formed a strange contrast to the mournful procession which was skirting along it. And so on through the Oval, across Vauxhall Bridge, up Grosvenor Place, along Piccadilly and at last to St. James's Square, which was reached towards two o'clock in the morning. About thirty individuals had collected outside No. 14—the house was at the north-east corner of King Street and the Square—but, according to an onlooker 'they were evidently of the lower orders of society.'

Inside the house, on the ground floor, a room, known as the yellow room and used as a writing-room, had been prepared for a brief lying-in-state. The room had been completely lined with superfine cloth and hung with six silver sconces, each bearing two wax candles. At one end, against the wall, there was a large diamond-shaped hatchment on which were emblazoned Castlereagh's arms, with their motto *Metuenda corolla draconis*. Resting on trestles was a larger state coffin, in which the smaller coffin was now deposited and the lid screwed down. This was covered with rich Genoa velvet and richly decorated with gilt ornaments consisting of coronets enclosed in panels with silver stars. A black velvet pall, trimmed with a treble flounce of satin, was then thrown over the catafalque. Several rich plumes of sable ostrich-feathers were then placed on top of the coffin, each plume being surmounted by a small streamer, terminating in a point, on which was painted a coronet. Castlereagh's own coronet was laid on a crimson velvet cushion at the head of the coffin. On each side stood three immense wax candles in massive silver candlesticks. The whole, so we are informed, was 'judiciously arranged' by the efficient Mr. Newton, and 'presented an appearance of mournful grandeur'.

Throughout the remainder of the night, watch was kept over the bier by two of the household servants, who had accompanied the procession from North Cray.

For some days past, anonymous notices had been placarded over London urging that the body of a suicide should not be allowed to defile the sanctuary of Westminster Abbey. The authorship of these notices is unknown, but there is no doubt that, in conjunction with some bitter newspaper articles attacking the late Minister's political character and reputation from the pen of the Radical William Cobbett, they had the effect of stirring up public feeling. During the preceding days a hostile crowd had collected outside the house in St. James's Square, shouting offensive remarks. The original intention was that everyone attending the funeral should be invited to accompany the hearse from the house to the Abbey, but in view of these demonstrations it was decided to restrict the procession to a few close friends, besides the pall-bearers and relatives. This annoyed Princess Lieven, the wife of the Russian Ambassador. 'It is a half measure, a piece of cowardice,' she wrote to her lover the Austrian Chancellor, Prince Metternich, 'a thing one sees here only too often.'

The coaches and carriages which made up the funeral procession began to arrive in St. James's Square soon after six o'clock in the morning. The footmen and coachmen received their instructions from Mr. Newton and were provided with black silk hatbands and gloves. A little later the friends and relatives assembled in the drawing-room, where they were handed mourning scarves as well as hatbands and gloves. They also had an opportunity of viewing the lying-in-state.

The procession formed up at 8.30 a.m. and moved off a few minutes later. First came several police officers, including the High Constable of Westminster, wearing a mourning cloak and cocked hat and carrying his silver staff of office. Three mourning coaches followed, containing the eight pall-bearers, who were all members of the Cabinet (Lords Liverpool, Eldon, Sidmouth and Stowell, the Dukes of Wellington and Marlborough, and Messrs. Frederick Robinson and Nicholas Vansittart). Immediately in front of the hearse rode a man on horseback carrying Castlereagh's coronet. The hearse itself was drawn by six horses, with luxuriant plumes of black ostrich-feathers, each led by a page. There followed ten carriages, carrying various nobility and gentry. The first included, besides the chief mourner, Frederick, Lord Castlereagh, the Bishop of London and the Speaker of the House of Commons. The last carriage carried three individuals who had been closely associated with the dead man. They were his physician, Dr. Bankhead; his solicitor, Mr. Groom; and the artist Sir Thomas Lawrence, who had painted his portrait on at least four occasions.

This small but impressive cavalcade passed out of St. James's Square into Pall Mall, along Cockspur Street, past Charing Cross and down Whitehall to Parliament Square. The crowd which accompanied it and lined the route at various places behaved in quite an orderly manner until the hearse reached the West Door of the Abbey. Here there was a slight pause to enable the coffin to be removed from the hearse and hoisted on to the shoulders of the pall-bearers. At this moment several people in the crowd began to shout 'Hurrah!' and wave their hats, at which the Duke of Wellington held up his hand and said 'Hush'. There were a few cries of 'Shame!' but they were soon drowned in the general cheering. And so to the mingled sound of cheers, groans and hisses and the waving of hats, the coffin was quickly borne into the Abbey and the door closed on the exulting mob outside. It was a disgraceful scene. Some of those within mistook the sounds, which could be distinctly heard, as a greeting for the Duke. 'If this be a compliment, it is a very ill-judged one,' remarked a peer in the congregation who thought it might have been intended as a mark of respect, instead of the reverse. The noise reminded one Tory politician of the welcome which Castlereagh received when he attended the King's Coronation only a year previously, although its volume on the occasion of the funeral surprised him. 'In tone it was a little different from the applause with which Lord Londonderry was last received in the same place,' wrote John Wilson Croker, 'when that which is now a corpse was the second figure in the most splendid ceremony that this country ever saw. I had been all along apprehensive of some insults, and had used my little endeavour to persuade the friends to have an earlier and more private funeral. I confess I apprehended only a scattered disapprobation, groans or perhaps hisses; but the loud acclamation of joy from a considerable body of people I was totally unprepared for.'

Another Ministerial colleague, Henry Hobhouse, did not consider the malcontents on this occasion to be so numerous as represented by Croker, although he shared the latter's view that a private funeral would have been more appropriate in the circumstances, particularly as Castlereagh's youngest and favourite sister Octavia was buried in the parish church in Cray,* and the dead statesman was supposed to have expressed the desire at the time that his remains might eventually repose beside hers with those of his wife. 'Many sober-minded persons thought that, considering the manner of his death, it would have been more judicious to give him a private funeral at Cray,' Hobhouse recorded in his journal at the time. 'And the circumstance of his having desired, when his sister Lady Ellenborough was buried there, that there should be space in the vault for him, induced a belief that he designed it for the sepulchre of himself and his wife. The only friend consulted was Lord Clanwilliam, who seemed rather to participate in Lady Londonderry's views on the subject, and did not resort to the argument arising from the circumstances just stated, the only argument perhaps which in the existing state of Her Ladyship's mind could with delicacy and propriety be urged against a funeral in the Abbey.'

'Whatever were the sentiments of anyone with regard to the place of interment,' Hobhouse continued, 'no one doubted about paying his respect to the memory of the deceased; and all the Foreign Ministers and about a hundred official men and members of the two Houses of Parliament attended, notwithstanding the shortness of the notice. A feeling of regret was very general even among the crowd, and though men had been so lavish of their abuse of him when living, there was no insult offered to his remains except by a small knot of men, who when the coffin was taken out of the hearse at the Abbey door raised three Huzzahs but were not joined by the bystanders.'

A grave had been opened in the north transept near the statue of the great Chief Justice, Lord Mansfield. Here the

*Lady Octavia Stewart, who was born in 1792, married in 1813 the Hon. Edward Law, later Earl of Ellenborough. She died in 1819.

clergy and mourners, including the whole diplomatic corps, ranged themselves in a semicircle. The Dean of Westminster read the Psalm, but the lesson was omitted in order to shorten the service. At twenty minutes to ten the coffin was lowered into the grave, the scene being described by Lord Liverpool, the Prime Minister, as 'particularly solemn and awful'. The choristers chanted, 'Man that is born of a woman hath but a short time to live and is full of misery'. The hoary old Lord Chancellor, Lord Eldon, began to weep while, according to the United States Minister, Richard Rush, he never saw 'manly sorrow more depicted in any countenance than that of the Duke of Wellington', who also stood by the vault. 'Earth to earth, ashes to ashes, dust to dust,' intoned the Dean, as a gentleman with a small lacquered spade and a bag threw some earth into the grave. The service ended with the choir singing 'I heard a voice from Heaven'. The congregation then dispersed in silence.

A few weeks afterwards the Whig M.P., John Cam Hobhouse, later Lord Broughton, met the poet Lord Byron in Italy; Byron told him that he had 'written against Castlereagh', and Hobhouse advised him to be cautious as to 'how he touched on his death'. According to Hobhouse, Byron 'did not quite agree', though he seems to have taken the hint. At all events he confined his valedictory verses to the subject of the Abbey tomb. It must be admitted that they constitute one of the poet's less felicitous efforts.

> Posterity will ne'er survey
> A nobler grave than this:
> Here lie the bones of Castlereagh:
> Stop, traveller, and——!

However the departed statesman may have been regarded by Byron and the Radicals, there is no doubt that he was a great loss to his friends. One of them, Mrs. Harriet

Arbuthnot, visited the grave a few days after the funeral and shed some 'tears of bitterness and unavailing sorrow' on the cold stones over it. 'He lies by the side of Mr. Pitt,' she noted in her journal, 'among statesmen who may have surpassed him in brilliant talent, but not in those amiable and excellent qualities of the heart which constitute a good man and a good Christian.'

CHAPTER TWO

The King, the Bishop and the Duke

I

IT IS NOW POSSIBLE to reconstruct the sequence of events from the time the first serious signs of Castlereagh's mental breakdown began to appear. His Parliamentary Under-Secretary, Lord Clanwilliam, informed Lord Stewart on the day of the tragedy what he and one of his private secretaries, Hamilton Seymour, had noticed. 'We had as far back as eight or ten days ago remarked a certain, to him, unusual restlessness of mind,' he wrote, 'and a degree of restlessness about trifles entirely alien to his general disposition, such as to have said that he dreaded the responsibility of going to Verona, to have thought that there were plots against him, etc. Four days ago he said to Seymour that he felt himself overworked, "felt it here" pointing to his forehead. He also said to Seymour, putting his hand to his head, "My mind, my mind is, as it were, gone." '

The fact that something was amiss with the Foreign Minister became apparent to one or two of his friends on the previous Saturday week. On that day, 3rd August, Castlereagh gave a small political dinner at Cray. It was an all-male party, the guests consisting of members of the Government and including the Duke of Wellington, Charles Arbuthnot and John Wilson Croker, William Huskisson and Sir Robert Horton Wilmot. On entering the dining-room, the host asked the Duke to change places with him at table, without giving any particular reason, although their two covers had been laid side by side. During the meal Castlereagh complained to Wellington of having had rather a shock, when his horse threw him, coming down and cutting its knees. In general, however, he made light of the accident and the Duke considered that he was 'in particularly good spirits' at dinner. But the Duke also noticed that he drank rather more wine than usual. Indeed the wine was of excellent quality and, wishing to compliment him on it, Arbuthnot called out 'Lord Londonderry——'. Castlereagh immediately jumped to his feet and stood as if in expectation of something serious that was to follow. When he was told that it was about the wine they wished to speak to him, he sat down. But his manner was so strange that Huskisson remarked on it to Wilmot as they came away.

On this occasion there was a particular matter on which Arbuthnot wished to consult his host. Both he and his wife were close personal friends of the Castlereaghs and, besides this, Arbuthnot was Secretary to the Treasury and as such the Government Patronage Secretary and Chief Whip, so that he was in daily touch on business matters with the Foreign Minister. It so happened that for some time Arbuthnot had been receiving threatening letters from a man named Jennings, saying that if he did not get a job 'he would tell things he knew that would ruin many persons in office'. The letters were unsigned, but Arbuthnot knew the handwriting to belong to Jennings. After Jennings had been refused, another anonymous communication reached Arbuthnot, which he guessed had come from the same source although it was in printed form. It reached Arbuthnot on the morning of Castlereagh's dinner-party. This time the writer threatened to accuse Mrs. Arbuthnot of carrying on a love affair with the Duke of Wellington. There was no truth whatever in this accusation, and it naturally annoyed Arbuthnot very much and also his wife. After discussing the matter together, they both agreed that the best course would be to ask their friend what steps to take.

When Arbuthnot accordingly brought up the matter in private conversation, he was somewhat surprised that Castlereagh seemed to regard these anonymous letters as aimed at himself. The Patronage Secretary thought this rather peculiar at the time, knowing the contempt Castlereagh had always shown in the past for anonymous attacks. However, Castlereagh promised to see the Law Officers about the possibility of bringing a prosecution, and next day he wrote Arbuthnot a kind note advising his wife 'to treat such an attack with the contempt it deserved' and promising to call on her on Monday. 'Although I thought Lord Londonderry odd in his manner on the subject of these letters,' Wellington noted afterwards, 'I never saw him more decided or more clear in his mind. I saw a letter from him to Mr. Arbuthnot on the same subject the next day Sunday the 4th of August, in which he expressed himself with more than usual clearness and decision.'

In other respects, the dinner was a success and the host seemed his usual self. 'So happy did he appear,' wrote Croker ten days afterwards, 'so amiable, so contented with all about him, that we all congratulated him on having so well recovered from the fatigues of the session, which had evidently pressed heavily upon him for the last weeks of our sittings. Little could any of us see in that placid countenance, in that playful smile, in those outstretched hands spread to welcome us, the dreadful change that a few days were to make. Good God! What weak and wretched creatures are the wisest and best of us!'

Castlereagh drove up to town on Monday the 5th and as promised called to see Mrs. Arbuthnot. As soon as he came into the room, according to her account, he took her hand and entreated her 'in the most earnest manner' to tell him whether she had ever heard anything against him. He said he considered her as one of his greatest friends and that he thought she should have 'no false delicacy' in telling him if she had ever heard anything against his honour or his character. Mrs. Arbuthnot admitted afterwards that she was 'excessively astonished' at this behaviour and 'quite laughed at the idea of anything dishonourable against him'. She told him there and then that she had often heard that he was 'a great flirt and very fond of ladies', but that she did not suppose 'he would consider that as a great crime'. He seemed pleased at what she said and went on to tell her that about three years before he had received an anonymous letter 'threatening to tell of his having been seen going into an improper house' with a woman. It appeared that he was watched by a man, possibly the exigent Mr. Jennings or one of his blackmailing companions, who wrote next morning to the Minister, telling him what he had seen and asking for a job. Castlereagh took no notice of this communication and indeed thought no more about it until quite recently when, as Mrs. Arbuthnot gathered, more anonymous letters began to reach him on the same subject. At this moment Arbuthnot came in and his entry put an end to the conversation. Mrs. Arbuthnot then went off to an artillery display followed by fireworks and dancing, which was given by the Duke of Wellington at Woolwich Arsenal. Castlereagh and Arbuthnot agreed to come on later after they had seen the Law Officers, with whom Castlereagh had arranged a conference to discuss the anonymous letters.

The two men met the Attorney-General and the Solicitor-General as arranged in the afternoon. In one of the letters, it seemed, the writer had threatened to reveal Castlereagh's 'irregular conduct' to his wife, and in another the black-mailing scoundrel had accused him of what Mrs. Arbuthnot euphemistically described as 'a crime not to be named'. It is not known for certain what advice the Law Officers gave, but it is very likely that they recommended a prosecution.

Castlereagh and Arbuthnot then went on together to the Duke's party at Woolwich. Either before going or while he was there, Castlereagh sent a note to the French Ambassador, the Vicomte Chateaubriand, asking the Ambassador to call at St. James's Square at an unusually early hour on the following morning. This note considerably surprised the Ambassador, as it was not customary for the head of a foreign mission to be summoned personally by the Foreign Minister of the Court to which he was accredited except when the Minister had a personal message to deliver from the King. The normal practice for routine Ministerial conference was for the invitation to be sent through the *chef du protocol*.

However, in conformity with this message, His Excellency presented himself at the appointed hour next morning and sent up his name by a footman. But when the servant informed the Foreign Minister, who was in the act of dressing for the prorogation of Parliament, Castlereagh sent back word that he was receiving no visitors on that day. When he heard this, the Ambassador, thinking there was some mistake, asked the servant to remind his master that he had written for him to come. On the servant going up a second time and mentioning this fact, Castlereagh seemed suddenly to recollect himself, ordered that His Excellency should be shown up—but, strange to say, not to the drawing-room but to his dressing-room. The Minister uttered a few words of explanation, which helped to remove the awkwardness of the situation and convinced Vicomte Chateaubriand that no slight was intended towards him or his Court. Nevertheless he went on with his dressing and the incident struck the Ambassador as 'not a little extraordinary, Lord Londonderry being generally known as a nice observer of punctilio'. In the course of their conversation, which seems to have consisted of small talk, Chateaubriand congratulated the Foreign Minister on the approaching end of the parliamentary session. 'Yes,' said Castlereagh, 'it had to end or I should end.'

On his way to the prorogation of Parliament, Castlereagh again called on the Arbuthnots. On this occasion he spoke 'with great kindness' and sympathy of the attack made on Mrs. Arbuthnot, and stayed chatting until word was brought that the King had already left Carlton House. The Arbuthnot's were anxious that Castlereagh should return and dine with them after the prorogation, but Castlereagh begged to be excused, saying he had sent for his solicitor, Mr. Groom, and his principal private secretary, Mr. Planta, to talk about the anonymous letters. He promised to call again next day, before the Cabinet meeting which had been summoned for that morning, to say good-bye, as the Arbuthnots were leaving on Thursday for their country house in Northamptonshire and he would himself be leaving for the Continent shortly afterwards.

Some time later in the same day, after the prorogation of Parliament had taken place, Castlereagh attended a meeting which the Duke had summoned at the Ordnance Office 'to consider the means of reforming the commissariat in Canada'. Arbuthnot was among those present on this occasion. Wellington noted that the Foreign Minister 'took no part in the discussion and manifested no interest in it'. After the meeting broke up, Castlereagh stayed behind to talk to the Duke and Arbuthnot about the Jennings letters. Wellington thought that he showed that he felt more about them than he had on the preceding Saturday, 'but there was no appearance of agitation respecting them'.

The next day was Wednesday 7th August. Castlereagh called on the Arbuthnots in the morning and stayed for some time. Mrs. Arbuthnot had a presentiment of evil; she recorded later that she was 'excessively out of spirits' and cried almost the whole time Castlereagh was with her. He seemed affected by her tears and asked her if she was displeased with him and whether he had ever offended her. ('God knows he never had,' noted Mrs. Arbuthnot in her journal.) They had some further conversation about the anonymous letters, particularly the one relating to her and the Duke of Wellington. Throughout their meeting, he held her hand, kissed it repeatedly and did all he could to cheer her spirits. When he left for the Cabinet, he stood for a few moments by the door and told her he was going down to Cray that evening, but would be coming up again next day and would call early to see her then before she left with her husband for the country. Thus 'he would put off the evil hour of saying good-bye'.

In fact, as will be seen, they never did meet again. 'Alas!', wrote Mrs. Arbuthnot afterwards, 'I dwell on these minute details with melancholy pleasure; they are my last remembrances of a friend I loved more than a brother. . . . He went, and the door closed for ever on my dear and valued friend.'

2

The Cabinet room had begun to fill up by the time Castlereagh reached Downing Street. It was on the whole a mediocre collection of fifteen individuals, of whom no less than nine belonged to the House of Lords. Of those in the Commons only Mr. Robert Peel, the Home Secretary, and Castlereagh himself possessed any marked abilities. The remainder included such mediocrities as the Chancellor of the Exchequer, Mr. Nicholas Vansittart, later Lord Bexley, and the President of the Board of Trade, Mr. Frederick John Robinson, later Viscount Goderich and Earl of Ripon, 'the transient and embarrassed phantom' of Disraeli's celebrated phrase in *Endymion*. Among the peers the 'archmediocrity', to quote Disraeli again, was the Prime Minister, Lord

Liverpool. Of the remainder, which included Lords Eldon, Westmorland, Harrowby and Sidmouth, only the Duke of Wellington was at all conspicuous for meritorious achievement.

The Cabinet meeting had been summoned for the purpose of going over the instructions which the Foreign Secretary had prepared for himself at the approaching conference of Heads of States and their Foreign Ministers, which it had been arranged should take place in the following month in Verona. The ostensible purpose was to discuss Italian affairs, but its real object was to consider the situation of Spain, particularly as affected by her former colonies in Latin America, who had recently thrown off the yoke of the Mother Country and proclaimed their independence. Castlereagh had already explained to his Cabinet colleagues that he proposed to get out in about a week, first spending a few days in Paris and then going on to Vienna, where he planned to have some preliminary conversations with Prince Metternich, as well as with the Austrian and Russian Emperors, before the conference proper assembled in Verona. According to the Duke of Wellington, the Prime Minister read the instructions to the assembled Cabinet. Means must be found, Castlereagh had written, even for the sake of Spain herself, 'of restoring an intercourse where she cannot succeed in re-establishing a dominion'. Britain had in effect already accorded *de facto* recognition to the former Spanish colonies as independent states. 'The practical question then,' wrote Castlereagh, 'is, how long should the *de facto* system of recognition be maintained to the exclusion of the diplomatic, and when should the latter be adopted?' The answer to this question the Minister felt must depend upon circumstances, and Castlereagh proposed that the British Government should reserve to itself full discretion to act according to its view of them. 'It will be the duty of the British Plenipotentiary to enter into discussion with the

Allied Cabinets, endeavouring as far as possible to bring them to the adoption of common sentiments, but taking care in every alternative to leave to the British Government an independent discretion to act according to circumstances.'

After Lord Liverpool had read over Castlereagh's instructions, there was some discussion on them. But the Foreign Minister took no part in the discussion. 'He appeared very low, out of spirits and unwell,' Wellington observed. 'There was, however, no appearance of agitation.'

When the Cabinet dispersed, Castlereagh went across to the Foreign Office for a short time, while Wellington paid another call in Downing Street. A little later, the Duke met the Foreign Minister 'as he was coming out of the back door of his office'. (This led on to St. James's Park.) Together they walked across the Park as far as Castlereagh's house in St. James's Square. Castlereagh seemed preoccupied: 'remarkably low and silent', and indeed, as he subsequently told the Duke, he imagined from his manner that Wellington 'had heard something against him and believed it'. According to the Duke, Castlereagh held him by the arm and scarcely said a word. Wellington left him at his door and then returned to the Ordnance Office. About half an hour later, the Duke went to Carlton House to pay his respects to the King, as he was shortly leaving for his annual tour of inspection of the Netherland fortresses. He found Castlereagh at Carlton House and, as the King was out, they walked back together through St. James's Square, Wellington leaving his friend at his house as before. About an hour later the two men met for the third time. Wellington had occasion to go to his own house and, as he was returning from Apsley House to the Ordnance Office, he encountered the Duke of York who was driving a buggy in The Mall. He stopped to speak to him and a few minutes later Castlereagh rode up on horseback and joined them. Wellington left them together. 'He then appeared very low and out of spirits.'

On getting back to St. James's Square, Castlereagh found one of his private secretaries, a young man and kinsman named Hamilton Seymour, whom he had invited to dine with him, waiting with some boxes of incoming dispatches which had come over from Downing Street. They then dined together and after dinner the two men drove down together to Cray. During the journey the private secretary read over the various dispatches to his chief, who gave his instructions as to how they should be answered 'with clearness and precision'. At the same time Hamilton Seymour thought he appeared 'deeply dejected' and also 'more humble' than usual. 'When I ventured to set up my opinion against his,' the secretary recalled afterwards, 'he at once acquiesced in my suggestions, and I cannot perhaps better describe his state than by saying that he showed more deference to my opinion and seemed to have less confidence in his own than was habitual to him.'

Most of the next day, which was Thursday, Castlereagh seems to have spent moping about the grounds at North Cray. He was seen walking at a heavy lifeless pace, at one moment with his eyes fixed on the ground and at another moment gazing at the heavens. Hamilton Seymour saw him go by himself towards the river at the foot of the grounds and 'there was something so melancholy and dejected in his manner' that the private secretary resolved to follow him and 'if possible by conversing with him to draw him out of the state of gloomy reflexion in which he appeared to be absorbed'. After vainly endeavouring to make him talk about some other subjects, Hamilton Seymour mentioned their approaching journey to Vienna.

"I hope, Lord Londonderry, that you are looking forward with pleasure to our Continental trip," said the private secretary. "The journey will, I think, be of use to you, as you will have the satisfaction of renewing several of your former diplomatic acquaintances?"

Castlereagh's reply was to draw his hand across his forehead and say very slowly, "At any other time I should like it very much, but I am quite worn out *here*." He still kept his hand on his forehead, as he went on. "Quite worn out— and this fresh load of responsibility now put upon me is more than I can bear."

Much as he was surprised at 'this sort of confession of apprehension', so unlike the language and conduct usually employed by his chief, Hamilton Seymour was much more alarmed at 'the nervous and querulous tone in which it was uttered'. Next day he confided in his father, Lord George Seymour, who had come to stay at Cray, that he knew his chief well enough to be sure that these fears and the tone in which they were expressed proved that 'something was very much amiss with him'.

On this day, Friday 9th August, Castlereagh, accompanied by his wife, drove up to town early as he had several appointments, including an audience with the King who was going on a visit to Scotland; the Foreign Minister wished to take leave of His Majesty. Shortly before noon he was seen walking along Pall Mall 'in a very abstracted manner', and with the top of one of his boots falling over his ankle, as if regardless of his personal appearance. He wandered into Cockspur Street, past the British Coffee House, where the proprietor happened to be standing in the doorway. Castlereagh went up to him and inquired for an acquaintance named Sir Edmund Nagle. On being informed that he was not there, his lordship, according to an observer, struck his hands together 'with much emotion' and 'very sharply desired that some of the other waiters should be called'. It was with some difficulty that the waiters were able to persuade him that Sir Edmund was not concealed in the house. Eventually Castlereagh walked away 'very much agitated', while his conduct appeared 'very singular' to several passers-by and 'excited particular attention in the street'.

He now turned back towards St. James's Street and in so doing was pointed out to a gentleman who had never seen him before, but whose curiosity was so much aroused at this first sight that he determined to follow him and 'have a complete stare at one whose participation in the political changes in Europe during the last twenty years had been so prominent'. Accordingly he closely pursued his steps up St. James's Street and into Piccadilly, where, to his great surprise, he saw his lordship mingle with the crowd which surrounded the coaches assembled in front of the White Horse Cellar. He then observed him approach a Jew boy, who had a tray of cheap knives which he was offering for sale. The Foreign Secretary, on looking them over, chose one with a white handle priced at one shilling, which he immediately put in his waistcoat pocket, and throwing down the money walked away. The gentleman, who remarked this transaction, thought it singular at the moment that 'so great a man should deal in so small a way', and at dinner the next day related the anecdote 'as a mark of the eccentricity which he did not expect to have discovered in a man of such high rank and consequence'.

It was apparently now time for the Foreign Minister's audience with the King, and so he made his way to Carlton House. But he did not immediately go in. He returned to his house in St. James's Square. In fact, he presented himself three times at Carlton House before he finally decided to enter. On turning back on one of these occasions, he remarked that he must first go to the Foreign Office before waiting upon the King. Finally, he went into Carlton House and was received by His Majesty in one of the private apartments.

He immediately seized the King by the arm.

"Have you heard the news, the terrible news?" asked Castlereagh, looking wild-eyed.

"No," replied the King. "What is it?"

"Police officers are searching for me to arrest me."

"Come, come," said the King, who thought at first that this was some kind of joke his Foreign Minister was playing on him. "What nonsense! Why should they be?"

"Because I am accused of the same crime as the Bishop of Clogher."

"You must be crazy."

Castlereagh looked deadly serious. "There is no doubt a warrant has been issued and they are looking for me," he went on. "I have just had my horses come up from Cray. I shall leave by the little gate in your garden. I shall go to Portsmouth and there sail for France. I can no longer live in England."

The King, who had been inclined to laugh at first, now assumed an air of severity.

"My lord, you forget yourself," he admonished him. "This pleasantry is misplaced."

But this had no effect on Castlereagh. "I know well that you are also my enemy," he continued. "Everyone hates me and shuns me. When I walk down the street, people take the opposite side to avoid meeting me. I am very unhappy." He then showed the King two anonymous letters he had received on the previous day. (According to Princess Lieven, the wife of the Russian Ambassador, who got the information direct from the King, the writer of one of these letters threatened to reveal his 'irregular conduct' to his wife, while the other letter 'concerned a more terrible subject'. It was this second letter, in her opinion, that had sent him off his head.)

The King thereupon took him by both hands, felt his pulse, and begged him to compose himself. "Come, my dear

Londonderry," he said. "Have yourself bled and chase away your fit of blue devils. Remember the old times! Do you think you have a better friend than I?"

At this the unfortunate Foreign Minister buried his head in his hands and wept. "I am mad," he replied between sobs. "I know I am mad. I have known it for some time, but no one has any idea of it."

Again he seized the King's arm. "Promise me to keep this a secret to yourself alone," he went on wildly. "Swear to me, not on your oath as a King, but as an honourable man, that you will not breathe a word of this to any of my colleagues—in fact to no one—but above all *never* to my colleagues. I shall not leave until you have given me your word."

The King promised. But at the same time he insisted that Castlereagh should see his doctor without delay and that he should be bled. His Majesty then followed the ailing Minister into the adjacent ante-room, where there were several equerries and others in attendance. "What's the matter with Londonderry?" he whispered to one of them. "Either he is mad, or I am."

The Foreign Minister appeared a little calmer when he took his leave a few minutes later. But he still chattered away about the Bishop of Clogher, convinced that he was 'fugitive from justice' and that he must 'fly to the ends of the earth'.

The King mentioned his European trip. "Sire," replied Castlereagh, with the utmost solemnity. "The time has come to say good-bye to Europe. You and I alone have known Europe, and together we have saved her. There is no one left after me with any knowledge of Continental affairs."

As he looked at the departing visitor, so His Majesty afterwards recalled, he had a premonition of approaching tragedy. "My own mind was then filled with apprehensions respecting him," he told Lord Eldon, "and they have, alas, been but too painfully verified."

In the ante-room of Carlton House, as Castlereagh passed through on his way out, a gentleman named John Beckett happened to be waiting. Mr. Beckett saw the Foreign Minister and remarked to him casually, "So you purpose leaving us for the Congress?"

"Purpose?" exclaimed Castlereagh, glowering at the questioner. "So you are in the conspiracy against me, to prevent me going?"

Mr. Beckett was so astonished that he could not make any reply, and the Minister walked on without another word.

3

During the previous three weeks the affair of the Bishop had made a considerable stir in London. Indeed it was a prime topic of conversation in the clubs and coffee-houses, although from the nature of the case its details were scarcely fit to be discussed in drawing-rooms. Public interest was increased by the fact that the accused person was not only a high dignitary of the Church but also a member of an aristocratic Irish family and the uncle of a peer. The Right Rev. Percy Jocelyn, Bishop of Clogher, was the third son of the first Earl of Roden, a landowner whose estates by a curious coincidence were situated not far from Castlereagh's ancestral property in County Down. Although it was a suffragan bishopric, nevertheless Clogher boasted a fine episcopal palace, also in Ulster, which the Bishop had occupied for the past two years. Before that he had for over a decade been Bishop of Ferns. He was about fifty-seven years of age and was unmarried.

On the night of the 19th July 1822, his lordship, who was

in London on a visit from Ireland, went into a public-house called the White Hart in St. Alban's Place, Westminster. There he was detected in the act of committing a homosexual offence with a private soldier of the 1st Regiment of Guards, named John Moverley. He was attired in his customary episcopal dress and made no attempt to conceal the nature of his calling. 'The Bishop took no precautions,' noted Charles Greville in his diary at the time, 'and it was next to impossible he should not have been caught. He made a desperate resistance when taken, and if his breeches had not been down they think he would have got away.' He was then escorted along with the soldier to the watch-house in Vine Street, being followed by a crowd, which shouted insulting remarks after them as they went along. Arrived in Vine Street, he refused to give his name to the constable of the watch. But his indentity was revealed by a letter, which he took out of his pocket and tore up. He threw the fragments into the fire-place, but as there was no fire burning there, they were recovered by the constable and pieced together. The letter turned out to be from his nephew, Lord Roden. This was confirmed by a note which he asked the constable to send to a friend in the house where he lodged off Portman Square, in which he wrote that he was 'totally undone' and signed himself 'P C ', the initial letters of his christian name and diocese.

Next day the two delinquents were brought before the local magistrate, and after they had been formally charged they pleaded not guilty and reserved their defence. The magistrate informed them that their offences were bailable, and he fixed the amount of bail each in £500 and two sureties in £250 each. Two sureties came forward on behalf of the Bishop and entered into the necessary recognisances The Bishop was thereupon released, though not until he had given his name and address, which he did with considerable reluctance. No sureties appeared for the soldier, so that the unfortunate Private Moverley was remanded in custody.

Meanwhile the affair continued to be talked about and the people of the public-house made a good deal of money by showing the place. According to Greville, Lord Sefton went to see the soldier in prison. 'He says he is a fine soldier-like man and has not the air which these wretches usually have. . . . It seems that the soldier will be proceeded against with the greatest vigour, and the Magistrate is much blamed for having taken such small bail as that which he required. The Duke will not spare the soldier. Lord Lauderdale said the other day that the greatest dissatisfaction would pervade the public mind at the escape of the Bishop and the punishment of the soldier, and the people, who cannot discriminate, or enter into nice points of law, will only see in such apparent injustice a disposition to shield an offender in the higher classes of society from the consequences of his crime, while the law is allowed to take its course with the more humble culprit. He said he would have exacted the greatest bail of the Bishop that ever had been taken. . . .'

As it happened, this was not the first time that the Bishop had been accused of attempting to commit such an offence. Eleven years previously in Dublin a domestic servant named James Byrne had charged his lordship with having made an immoral proposition to him. For this the servant was prosecuted for criminal libel by the Bishop, and on his conviction was sentenced to two years' imprisonment and also to be publicly flogged. The latter punishment was carried out with such severity that the poor man nearly died. This incident was now recalled in connection with the Bishop being granted such lenient bail, particularly when the fears expressed by Greville and others were abundantly justified and the Bishop failed to appear to stand his trial at the next sessions at Clerkenwell.

While preparations were being made to deprive the Bishop of his ecclesiastical dignities, he broke his bail and fled to Scotland, where he anticipated there would be difficulties in executing any warrant for his re-arrest. Here he assumed the name of Thomas Wilson and for a time, it is said, took employment as a butler, on one embarrassing occasion being recognised by one of his former acquaintances as he was handing round the dishes at dinner. He died incognito in Edinburgh in 1843 and had a very different funeral from Castlereagh's. He was buried quietly in the new cemetery, at seven o'clock in the morning, followed by only five mourners in a one-horse coach. By his directions no name appeared on his coffin, but the plate bore an inscription in Latin, which he had himself devised some years previously. The translation read: 'Here lies the remains of a great sinner, saved by grace, whose hope rests in the atoning sacrifice of the Lord Jesus Christ.'

4

To return to the Foreign Secretary. About four o'clock in the afternoon of 9th August the Duke of Wellington happened to be riding through St. James's Square on his way home from the Ordnance Office, prior to setting out for the Continent. As he passed his colleague's house, Lady Castlereagh, who was looking out of the window, called to him and he stopped to talk to her. While the Duke was thus engaged in passing the time of day, Castlereagh himself returned on foot from his extraordinary interview with the King at Carlton House. The Duke noticed that he was walking 'in rather a quick and hurried pace'. As the Foreign Secretary passed him, he told the Duke that he wanted to speak to him. The Duke accordingly followed him into the house and to his room.

Castlereagh motioned the Duke towards a sofa and they

sat down together. Then he began to talk about the unfortunate Bishop of Clogher and his offence, still imagining that he had been accused of a similar crime. He said that all his friends, including the Duke, had conspired against him, that somebody had sent his horses up to town that he might fly, and that it was necessary for him to do so. He told the Duke a strange and confused story to the effect of a man telling him, as he was coming out of Carlton House, that his horses were waiting for him, of his not having ordered his horses to town and of the arrival of the horses, and of his being informed of their arrival, as proof that the person who had ordered up his horses and the person who told him that they were waiting thought there was so much against him that he ought to fly the country.

"To prove to you what danger I am in, my own servants think so, and that I ought to go off directly—that I have no time to lose—and they keep my horses saddled that I may get away quickly. They think I should not have time to go away in a carriage."

"Depend upon it," said the Duke, "this is all an illusion. Your stomach is out of order. Ring the bell and ask if your horses are in London. Convince yourself!"

At this Castlereagh jumped up and gave the bell-rope a violent pull. The servant was rather slow in answering, so that Castlereagh stamped on the ground and pulled the rope again, this time with such force that it broke. When at last the servant appeared, his master shouted at him harshly.

"Who dared to order my horses up to town?"

"They are not in town, my lord," the man replied. "They have not been ordered. They are at Cray."

When he heard these words, Castlereagh turned towards the Duke. "There's not even a servant who is faithful to me," he said. "Everyone is my enemy, and you're the first of them all."

"You're mad," exclaimed the Duke. As the servant left the room he added, "There! You see it's as I said."

Castlereagh thereupon flung a handkerchief over his face, sank back on the sofa, and burying his head in his hands burst into tears.

"Yes, I know I am mad, quite mad," he sobbed. "And since you say so, it must be so."

"Now then, you've got an attack of fever," said the Duke. "I'm going to look for your doctor. Go back to the country and nurse yourself there for a few days. Get yourself ready for the Continental journey. The trip will do you good. I shall postpone my own departure for a day or two, and stay near you till you leave."

The Duke, who as we have seen was about to set out for the Netherlands, had arranged to drive down to Dover that night so as to embark on the following morning.

To the suggestion that the Duke should put off his journey, Castlereagh was strongly opposed. "If you stay with me," he told his friend, "your motive will be discovered and my name will be covered with shame. On the contrary, you must promise me to leave tomorrow."

The Duke gave his word and, after extracting a promise from Castlereagh on his side that he would see his doctor, Wellington went off in search of Dr. Bankhead himself. Not finding him at home, he returned to Apsley House and wrote Bankhead the letter which was subsequently read out by the Coroner at the inquest and which has been already quoted. This was immediately taken round to Dr. Bankhead's house by hand.

Wellington also wrote an account of what had happened to his friend Arbuthnot, who had now gone off with his wife to the country.

London. August 9th 1822. I am just setting off, but I cannot go without making you acquainted with the impression made upon my mind by an interview I have just had with Lord Londonderry. It appears that his mind and body have been overpowered by the work of the session, and that he is at this moment in a state of mental delusion. He took me into his house to talk to me about the same story that he told to you and Lord Liverpool; and strange to say he imagined from my manner at the last Cabinet, and afterwards walking home with him, that I believed it. He thought the same of the Duke of York. . . .

He is certainly very unwell; and I did not conceal from him my opinion that he was so, and that his mind was not in its usual and proper state. I offered to stay with him: but he would not allow me, as he said it would make people believe there was some reason for it. I begged him to send for Dr. Bankhead: and between ourselves I have informed Dr. Bankhead that in my opinion he is labouring under a temporary delusion. He cried excessively while talking to me and appeared relieved by it, and by his conversation with me; and he promised me to see Bankhead.

I am afraid that he has mentioned his story of [his being accused of the same crime as the Bishop of Clogher]* to more persons than Lord Liverpool, you and me. I have entreated him to say no more about it to anybody; but I fear he will.

I write you all this in order to urge you to see him as soon as you can after you will return to London; and observe him well and see whether his mind is quite right. If it is not, and he should go abroad, I think you ought to make him take Bankhead with him: and if that is not

*In the original MS. letter, in the possession of the present Duke of Wellington, who has kindly supplied me with a copy, the writer has used the figure 19 as a cypher at this point, which I have taken to mean the words enclosed in the brackets.

accomplished, I think you ought to mention the matter to Planta. Otherwise it is my opinion that this impression of mine should never go beyond our little Cabinet.

He is quite clear and right about publick matters; but agreed with me that his mind had been overpowered by his work of the session and that he was labouring under a delusion!

Meanwhile the King, who could not get the distressing picture of his Foreign Minister off his mind, sent an urgent note in his own handwriting by messenger to St. James's Square, marked 'Private' and 'Immediate'. 'Dear Londonderry,' wrote His Majesty, 'I was so very uneasy at the state of feverishness under which you were labouring when I saw you this morning, that I cannot rest until you have written me word that you have seen Dr. Bankhead before you return into the country. Or, if you cannot meet with him, pray send, I conjure of you, for my friend Sir William Knighton.' The note ended, 'ever your affectionate friend, G.R.'

Castlereagh's wife also sent a note to Dr. Bankhead, who appears to have received it before the Duke's. About the same time, the Foreign Secretary was conversing somewhat aimlessly with Prince Lieven, the Russian Ambassador, and M. Werther, the Prussian Minister, who had called on him at his house by appointment. He told them that he felt his brain was disturbed ('*Jessens mon cerveau ebranlé*'), but as they were accustomed to his rather peculiar French they did not pay much attention to what he said. They thought he merely had a headache. Later, when he was being bled by the cupper, Bankhead noticed that 'the blood came away as thick as glue'. This latter symptom was confirmed by the Minister's wife, who wrote a note to the Duke before leaving for Cray with her husband.

London,
9th August, 1822

Dear Duke,

From your kind feeling with respect to Lord Londonderry, I am sure you will be glad to hear that he saw Bankhead, who ordered him to be cupped. The blood resembled jelly, and he was instantly relieved, and I have hopes that he will be well in a few days, but I really think he was on the verge of brain fever.

Yours most sincerely,
E. A. LONDONDERRY

It was nearly four o'clock in the morning when Wellington reached Dover. The packet was waiting and he went on board without delay, but like the King he could not dismiss the image of Castlereagh from his mind, and he sent a note to Mrs. Arbuthnot on the subject as soon as he had disembarked at Calais.* 'I cannot describe to you the impression it has made on me,' he wrote. 'To see a man with such a sober mind, who one would think could not be influenced by any illusion, in a state bordering upon insanity, is not calculated to raise one's opinion of the strength of the human mind! Poor human nature! How little we are after all!' Wellington added that Castlereagh was aware of his state, which he did not conceal from him. 'I am certain that he will not be able to go abroad this week, if he should be able to go at all. I am equally certain that he will recover entirely.'

About the same time as Wellington reached Calais, King George IV was embarking on the Royal Yacht at Woolwich for his voyage to Scotland. He had sent Lord Liverpool an urgent message in the middle of the night to come to Woolwich as soon as he could. Having already had his farewell

*Wellington MSS. (Communicated by courtesy of the Duke of Wellington).

audience of His Majesty, the Prime Minister was at a loss to understand the reason for this summons. When he duly presented himself, the King asked him if he had guessed why he had sent for him. Liverpool replied that he had not the slightest idea.

"When did you last see Lord Londonderry?"

"On Wednesday at the Cabinet."

"How was he?"

"As usual, very well."

"Well," said the King. "I tell you that he's mad, quite mad, and if he is not watched, he is capable of making an attempt on his life. It's impossible for me to put off my departure, otherwise I would take on myself the wretched job of watching him. But I count on you. See to it that something is done. Speak to those who are closest to him, and above all take care that he's not left alone for a moment."

Knowing what he described as the King's 'tendency to exaggeration', Lord Liverpool did not attach a great deal of importance to what was said on this occasion. Consequently the only action he took was to send a note to Cray the same day by a messenger asking the Foreign Minister to meet him in London after the week-end. To this Castlereagh's wife sent the following reply by return that evening.

North Cray,
Saturday [August 10, 1822]

Dear Lord Liverpool,

Lord Londonderry desires me to thank you for your communication. He is anxious to meet you in town on Monday, but he has been very unwell for some days and Doctor Bankhead (who is now here) says he must nurse himself up if he means to be ready to start for the Continent at the time settled.

I will trust to your good nature to forgive my asking you as a great favour to myself to come here either on

Monday or Tuesday, for I fear a journey to London would quite counteract the quiet nursing of this place. We can dine either day at any hour you please and shall be most happy if you will take a bed here. I again entreat you to forgive.

Believe me,

Yours very truly,

E. A. LONDONDERRY

Next morning the Prime Minister wrote to Lady Londonderry saying that he would certainly not press her husband to come to town and accepting her invitation. 'I will come down to him at Cray on Tuesday about an hour before dinner.' He added, 'You may therefore keep him quite quiet and let him recruit himself for his continental journey.'

If Lord Liverpool gave no hint of the King's orders and warning, Lady Londonderry on her side did not disclose to the Prime Minister how seriously ill her husband was. This is confirmed by several details which did not come out at the inquest. For instance, while driving down to Cray on the Friday evening with his wife, Castlereagh asked her, 'Did I speak much nonsense to the King today?' Then, recollecting that she could give no answer, he leaned back his head in the carriage and 'seemed sunk in a sort of lethargy'. Again at three o'clock on the Saturday morning he awoke in a fit of delirium and made his wife get up (for she continued to sleep with him) and bring him one of the red boxes out of the drawing-room below. He told her that the box contained papers 'on which his life depended'. But when she looked inside the box there were no papers of any importance there. Later in the morning his mind began to wander again. He made her read a novel to him and interrupted her reading several times, sitting up in bed and exclaiming, 'This is very extraordinary.' He seemed afraid he was being watched and asked his wife with great anxiety where his pistol-case was and whether she would give him the key.

This frightened Lady Londonderry. 'If you go on talking in this manner,' she said to him, 'I will go away and send Dr. Bankhead to you.'

As we have seen, Dr. Bankhead arrived in the late afternoon. He found his patient rather better from the effects of the medicine he had taken, 'but still there was heat and fever, great thirst, and an unusual watchfulness and suspicion of manner, and a constant anxiety lest he should not be well enough to go abroad in the appointed time'.*

In the evening he took a warm bath and apparently slept better. Next morning he expressed what Clanwilliam described as 'a forced and unnatural desire to shave', which again alarmed Lady Londonderry, who locked up his razors and anything else she could find in the room with which he might injure himself. At the same time she told her maid, Mrs. Robinson, to search the dressing-room thoroughly. Unfortunately Mrs. Robinson missed the knife, which he seems to have hidden in his dressing-case in a drawer in the washing-stand, having previously transferred it there from one of his dispatch-boxes. Whilst the rest of the household were at church on that Sunday, he talked incessantly to Bankhead, about plots and conspiracies, in the most despondent tone. He asked what people thought of him and whether they accused him of any crimes. The doctor begged him to be calm and not to talk of such things, as they excited him. The sick man replied that he could not go to the Continent as long as Bankhead 'allowed the suspicion of a crime to rest on him'.

He asked the doctor, 'How can you expect me to go to Vienna and exhibit myself to Europe and be present at a congress of sovereigns in the state I am?' The doctor did his

*From a statement by Bankhead written at Liverpool's request when he called on him at his house in London on the same day as Castlereagh died. It is reproduced, with other details, in Wellington, *Despatches, Correspondence and Memoranda*, 2nd Series, I, p. 254.

best to reassure him, and after a while he grew calmer.

Bankhead stayed with him all evening and left him about midnight 'tolerably comfortable'. During that night he got up twice and went into his dressing-room the first time to wash his face, and then, about an hour later, to clean his teeth, after which he returned quietly to bed. The last time he was to get up was early on the following morning, when, as we have seen, he passed Mrs. Robinson on his way to his dressing-room. 'Mrs. Robinson,' he said to her sternly, 'I will not be watched. Go and send Dr. Bankhead to me instantly.' In a few moments he was dead.

Too late a letter arrived for him from the King. It was written on 13th August after the Royal Yacht had been driven by a violent gale to take shelter in Berwick Bay. 'Let me entreat of you not to hurry your Continental journey until you feel yourself quite equal to it,' wrote King George. 'Remember of what importance your health is to the country, and above all things to me.'

CHAPTER THREE

Three Women

I

THERE WERE THREE WOMEN who played a prominent part in Castlereagh's life and in particular saw a great deal of him towards the end of it. The first of these was his wife, Emily, to whom he had been married for twenty-eight years. According to Lord Liverpool, to whom it will be remembered she had written two days before the final catastrophe, the Marchioness tended to minimise the seriousness of her husband's condition and to conceal as far as possible from the outside world how gravely ill he was. If the Prime Minister is to be believed, she was determined that the Continental journey, on which she was to accompany her husband, should not be cancelled or postponed and in consequence she made light of his indisposition, in the treatment of which she opposed 'with all her might' the proposal that Dr. Bankhead should call in a second opinion. Liverpool told Princess Lieven, the wife of the Russian Ambassador, that in an attempt to show that nothing much was wrong with Castlereagh she affected a forced gaiety, which was quite unusual with her, and even left him for the whole of the previous Saturday morning in order to go up from Cray to Greenwich and witness the King's departure for Scotland in the Royal Yacht. Whatever conclusions may be drawn from Lady Londonderry's behaviour in the days immediately preceding the tragedy, there seems no doubt that she was most anxious that the journey to Vienna should begin on the date planned. She had distinctly agreeable recollections of her last visit to the Austrian capital, at the time of the celebrated Congress, when as the wife of the British Foreign Minister and Special Envoy she had been made much of by Prince Metternich and the other Allied representatives.

There is no doubt too that Emily was deeply attached to her husband, the more so perhaps because they had no children. Indeed they appeared to observers to be a most happily married couple, an impression which is confirmed by Castlereagh's letters to her on the relatively few occasions when they were parted. 'I don't know what you feel,' he once wrote to her after many years of marriage when he was posting along the road to Ireland, having left her behind at Cray, 'but I am quite determined unless you differ never to pass from one country to another *even for a day* without you. You know how little I am given to professions, but I really of late felt your deprivation with an acuteness which is only known to those who are separated from what they most love. But I find I am in danger of committing the intolerable barbarism of writing a love-letter to my wife.'

When she left Blickling Hall, her beautiful family home in Norfolk, to marry the Hon. Robert Stewart, as he then was, in 1794, Lady Emily Ann Hobart, youngest daughter of John, 2nd Earl of Buckinghamshire, was a handsome young woman of twenty-two, with a strikingly attractive figure. Her physical attractions, however, had undergone a marked change with the passing years as she developed a decided stoutness. Indeed, her corpulence was a constant source of temptation to the wits and caricaturists of the day to indulge in unflattering comparisons at her expense, particularly as she had very thin legs. She was often eccentrically rather than fashionably dressed: on one occasion she astonished the assembled diplomatic corps at a ball in Vienna when she appeared wearing her husband's Order of the Garter

67

in her hair. She had no marked social tact, her conversation was far from brilliant, her taste in interior decoration bizarre, and her parties, which she gave regularly in St. James's Square after the opera on Saturday nights during the season, were generally considered to be rather dull affairs.

No one ever was so invariably good-humoured, yet she sometimes provokes me [wrote the Whig Lady Bessborough]; there is a look of contented disregard of the cares of life in her round grey eye that makes one wonder if she ever felt any crosses or knows the meaning of the word anxiety. She talks with equal indifference of bombardment* and assemblies, the baby and the furniture, the emptiness of London, Lord Castlereagh's increasing debility and the doubtful success of Mr. Greville's new opera—all these succeed each other so quick and with so exactly the same expression of voice and countenance that they probably hold a pretty equal value in her estimation.

Her most distinguishing feature was unquestionably her devotion to her husband. The Comtesse de Boigne, whose father was French Ambassador in London at this period, noted that she never left him at any time. 'While he worked, she was beside his desk,' she remarked. 'She followed him to town and to the country and accompanied him upon every journey . . . she would spend nights of cold, hunger and weariness in miserable lodgings without complaining or seeming to feel any inconvenience. In short, she did her utmost to be as little in the way as possible, throughout this apparent devotion. I say apparent, because their most intimate friends believed that in this respect she was following her own desires rather than those of Lord Castlereagh.

*This letter was written in September 1807, and the reference is to the bombardment of Copenhagen by the British fleet.

He, however, never offered any objection. I have sometimes thought in later years that she may have discovered some signs of that illness which was revealed to the world by the ultimate and dreadful catastrophe, and therefore desired to watch over him at all times and to relieve his sufferings. . . . Whatever the reason, Lady Castlereagh would never be separated an hour from her husband.' So far as political influence went, she exerted none whatever, nor apparently had she the slightest wish to do so.

They were perhaps happiest together among the flowers and gardens at Cray, where Emily had formed a small menagerie of beasts and birds and her husband raised a flock of merino sheep.

'The visitor's carriage drew up at a little gate,' noted the Comtesse de Boigne, 'and a walk between two beds of ordinary flowers led to a six-roomed house. One served as a drawing-room and study for the Minister, another for the dining-room, and the smallest as a cloak-room. On the first floor there were three bedrooms, one was appropriated to the Castlereaghs and the other two were reserved for guests . . . Lady Castlereagh had the good sense to lay aside her finery at Cray. She was to be found in a muslin dress, with a large straw hat on her head, an apron round her waist, a pair of scissors in her hand, cutting away dead flowers. Though the entrance to the house was exceedingly mean, it was situated in charming country and enjoyed a magnificent view: behind it there was a considerable enclosure, with rare plants, a menagerie and a kennel, which, with the greenhouses, divided the attention of Lady Castlereagh.'

Emily's zoo included an antelope, several kangaroos, emus and ostriches, and a tiger which Lord Combermere had brought from India for the Duke of Wellington and which the Duke had given to the mistress of Cray Farm. These animals were proudly displayed by Emily, although the tiger in particular did not welcome visitors. 'It seemed very vicious and growled at us,' noted Mrs. Arbuthnot when she and her husband first saw it. As for the merino sheep, their master won several prizes with them at agricultural shows. Castlereagh had taken a lease of this small property in 1811 for the term of his life and that of his wife, making extensive improvements to the place and considerably building on to the house, which was little more than a cottage, when he took it. Here he liked to entertain informally the members of the diplomatic corps and their wives, with whom he would converse in laboured and not always idiomatic French. Among them was Princess Lieven, who wrote to her lover, Prince Metternich, on 16th July 1820: 'Yesterday Lord Castlereagh showed me the changes he has had made in his country house. It has been much enlarged; but what taste in furnishing! The story of Don Quixote carpets his study, and Sancho is being tossed in a blanket just in front of his desk. He says that gives him a pleasant sensation, and he thinks its position is excellent. Join me in laughing!'

A frequent visitor to Cray Farm was Lady Castlereagh's niece, Lady Emma Edgecumbe, later Countess of Brownlow, who has given a vivid picture of the domestic scene there. She was a great favourite with Castlereagh, and as a girl of twenty-four she had accompanied the Foreign Minister and his wife to the Continent in 1814 and again in 1815, when they attended the various diplomatic proceedings which marked the concluding stages in the struggle against Napoleon. Of her uncle-by-marriage she was particularly fond. 'The calm dignity of his manner gave an impression that he was cold,' she wrote, 'but no one who had seen his kindly smile, or been greeted by his two hands stretched out in welcome, could have thought him so. To all those connected with him he was most affectionate. When his sister-in-law, Lady Catherine Stewart, was taken ill during the absence of his brother Charles with the army, he attended upon her constantly, gave her with his own hands her medicines and was with her when she died. He liked the society of young people and, far from checking their mirth and their nonsense, he enjoyed and encouraged it with his own fun and cheerfulness. His tastes were simple: he loved the country and a country life, and it was delightful to see his look of quiet happiness while taking a saunter after an early dinner in his pretty grounds at Cray and finishing with an evening ride or drive, often prolonged until after dark. On his return home he would sit down and write at the same table round which we all sat. If an air were played that pleased him, he would go to the pianoforte and sing it; if a waltz, he would say, 'Emma, let us take a turn,' and after waltzing for a few minutes he would resume his writing. His power of abstraction was indeed remarkable; our talking and laughter did not disturb him.'

Only once did Lady Brownlow recall that he ever was disturbed. That was one night when he rose from his chair laughing and saying, 'You are too much for me tonight.' He carried off his papers to what was called his own room, which was no doubt the room with the curiously designed carpet. But according to his niece he did not use this room much, preferring the general drawing-room as a rule. Next morning at breakfast he good-humouredly observed to the assembled company, 'You fairly beat me last night. I was writing what I may call the metaphysics of politics.'

Princess Lieven has left behind a rather more sophisticated description of an entertainment where the host partnered her in the dance which she is generally credited with having introduced into England. 'Yesterday,' she wrote to Metternich on 2nd August 1820, 'we were at a fête that Lord Castlereagh gave at his country place. We tried to be very gay. He himself insisted on waltzing with me—heavens, what hard work to keep the Minister in revolution! I am a very suitable person to make that kind of sacrifice, not as regards physical resources, but as regards goodwill. While we were dancing, those members of the party who had some sentimental preoccupation went for a stroll. It was a dark night; the little paths were well screened with thick laurel bushes; and the great majority of the guests gave us the slip. There were some comic scenes. In the end, the ball-room was occupied only by little girls, dancers of the calibre of my husband and the master of the house, a few old women and myself. Englishwomen always astonish me, in spite of my long experience of the country. I should like to take their indiscretion for the height of *naïveté*; but, after all, they have husbands, and I confess myself baffled.'

Neither Princess Lieven nor Mrs. Arbuthnot, Castlereagh's other close friend amongst his female acquaintances, was a particular favourite with Emily, as might perhaps be surmised. Towards each she bore feelings of jealousy and these feelings were to some extent reciprocated. While Mrs. Arbuthnot considered Emily unsympathetic and uninteresting, no doubt because politics bored her, Princess Lieven thought she was tactless and on one occasion downright stupid. She blamed her, as we shall see, for Castlereagh's falling out of favour with the King shortly before the catastrophe and for neglecting him at Cray during the last tragic forty-eight hours. 'He had nobody there but his wife,' she wrote to Metternich at the time, 'and what a wife!' Yet he never seems to have had any cause to reproach her for her conduct until within a few months of his death. He was devoted to his 'dearest Em' and left her completely provided for under his will. Besides a jointure of £2,200 a year, Emily also got the valuable diamonds which he had received as presents from the King and the other Allied sovereigns, with power to dispose of them in the possible event of a national emergency.

'My dearest Emily,' he wrote to her from Cray Farm in August 1818, 'political events in other countries have shaken private property (an event which in this happy country can hardly be apprehended), but as in such case I wish for your ease and comfort to be provided for in preference to all other considerations, I have therefore bequeathed to your absolute disposal the diamonds and beg you will not hesitate in such case to apply them to your own use. If the occasion should not occur, it is my wish then that they should be considered as memorials in the family of the public transactions, most of which you have shared with me as witness.'

2

Dorothea Christopherovna Lieven had first come to London in 1812, when her husband, Count (later Prince) Christopher Lieven had been appointed Russian Ambassador to the Court of St. James. She was then a dark, vivacious, witty and attractive young woman of twenty-seven from the Baltic provinces, with decided intellectual gifts as well as possessing a remarkable flair for politics and diplomacy. In a short time she had become an acknowledged leader of fashion and society, and a patroness of the exclusive Almack's Club, along with Lady Castlereagh. Among other achievements she has the credit for having introduced the waltz into English ballrooms. But in spite of the flattering likenesses from the brush of Sir Thomas Lawrence, she was never considered beautiful. Indeed her physical imperfections were the subject of contemporary comment. 'Strange to say, and in spite of her teeth, I admire her,' wrote Mr. Joseph Jekyll, one of the Regency men-about-town. 'I have never known her intimately enough to object to the effects said to be produced from her economy of clean linen.' In the English political scene she openly favoured the Tories, and was consequently on the most friendly terms with the leading members of Lord Liverpool's Government, as well as with the Prince Regent, later King George IV. For the Foreign Minister she had a real admiration and affection, although there can be little if any doubt that their relations were always what is generally known as platonic. With the Austrian Chancellor, however, she was on a different footing. At the Congress of Aix-la-Chapelle, in 1818, she had become Metternich's mistress. To this fortuitous circumstance we owe a most revealing series of letters from her to her lover, which contains many interesting details about English political and social life of the period, and in particular about the activities of the English Foreign Minister.

For many years the Prince Regent had been estranged from his wife, Caroline, and had lived with a succession of mistresses, of whom the most lasting was the Marchioness of Hertford. She was a discreet woman on excellent terms with the Ministry, and moreover was an aunt of Castlereagh's, a factor which made for harmony between Carlton House and Downing Street. But towards the end of 1819 the Regent's passion for his mistress, who was then sixty-three, began to wane, and with his accession to the throne as King George IV, early in the following year, Lady Hertford was displaced by the Marchioness of Conyngham. The new favourite, who was sixteen years younger than her predecessor, was a common, vulgar woman, and withal excessively mean and greedy. 'Not an idea in her head,' was Princess Lieven's penetrating comment, 'not a word to say for herself; nothing but a hand to accept pearls and diamonds, and an enormous balcony to wear them on.' She was on the worst possible terms with the Ministers in the Government, and with Lady Castlereagh in particular she was at daggers drawn. The result was that the King, who was by now completely infatuated with his latest lady-love, now ceased to invite his Ministers to dinner, although he had previously been on familiar terms with the whole Cabinet. The new monarch now began to think of turning out his Government and sending for the Whigs to form an administration instead.

The Foreign Minister was considerably disturbed by these developments, particularly by the change in royal favourites. 'Although we no longer live in the times when Mme de Pompadour directed the politics of Europe,' Princess Lieven wrote to Metternich at this time, 'I do not regard this London revolution as entirely without significance. Lord Castlereagh is a relative of the ex-favourite, and their connection put him on a more intimate footing with his master and gave him an added power. He is sulking now, and his sulks will strain their relations. One cannot tell what the ultimate effect will be.'

George IV's accession immediately raised the thorny question of his relations with his wife. In the past five years this unfortunate woman, now titular Queen, had been wandering round Europe, mostly in the company of an Italian named Bergami, officially her courier but generally believed to be her lover. During this period, George had, chiefly through the unwilling agency of Castlereagh and his brother, Lord Stewart, the Ambassador to Austria, been assiduously collecting evidence of Caroline's infidelities. As King he now demanded a divorce, but the Ministers, who were faced by a General Election in a few weeks, refused to agree and tendered their resignations in a body. The only alternative was a Radical Government, the prospect of which did not appeal to George. In the end he agreed that the Tories should remain in office on the understanding that no proceedings should be initiated against the Queen unless she returned to England. The dangerous tendencies of Radicalism were emphasised soon afterwards by the discovery of a plot, the so-called Cato Street Conspiracy, to assassinate the whole Cabinet while they were at dinner in Lord Harrowby's house in Grosvenor Square. Some of the Ministers were still in favour of resignation. 'We should have thrown up the whole thing twenty times over,' the Duke of Wellington told Princess Lieven, 'if Castlereagh and I had not represented to our colleagues what the general consequences would be if we resigned. We shall be firm: we must.'

Castlereagh had latterly become increasingly unpopular in the country. He had been blamed for the economic troubles and repressive legislation which followed the end of the Napoleonic wars and the return to a peace-time economy. Consequently the Cato Street conspirators nearly came to blows among themselves as to who should dispose of the Foreign Secretary. 'Everybody wanted the honour of cutting his throat,' noted Princess Lieven. Thereafter Castlereagh habitually carried two loaded pistols in his breeches pockets. One night, when the Russian Ambassador and his wife were dining with him at his house in St. James's Square, their host drew their attention to the pistols. 'He showed them to me at table,' she told Metternich afterwards. 'I was nervous every time he made a movement to offer me anything. I sat sideways in my chair; I edged away from the left and got so near to my right-hand neighbour that he could put nothing in his mouth without elbowing me.'

Unfortunately Queen Caroline returned to England and, as she refused to follow all suggestions that she should retire again to the Continent, the Ministers were obliged to redeem their promise and promote divorce proceedings in Parliament, where Castlereagh had the unpleasant task of introducing a Bill of Pains and Penalties designed both to dissolve her marriage and deprive her of her regal rights. To make matters worse for Castlereagh, the embarrassing Queen insisted on taking the house next door to his in St. James's Square. 'Here is a pretty piece of spite,' Princess Lieven remarked. 'Castlereagh told me that it would not disturb him in the least, except that the mob might begin to pull down his house. Few men have Lord Castlereagh's intrepid coolness, and more than once nothing but his unruffled appearance has overawed the mob.' That there was a real danger of the mob wrecking the Castlereagh mansion so long as its owner remained in it soon became apparent. A few days later Princess Lieven wrote: 'Lord Castlereagh has left his house; he was told that, however courageous it might be to brave the danger, his presence became criminal when it provoked a disturbance. So he has had his bed installed at the Foreign Office, in the room where he gives audience to ambassadors. To be reduced to that!'

Meanwhile Castlereagh's relations with the King went from bad to worse, because of the quarrel between the King's mistress and the Foreign Secretary's wife. According to Princess Lieven the trouble had started with some malicious remarks on the part of Lady Castlereagh about the reigning favourite. Lady Castlereagh announced that she would no longer invite Lady Conyngham to her evening receptions; the customary exchange of cards between them ceased, and the two women made a point of 'cutting' each other when they met anywhere in society.

In discussing the breach between them with his other friend Mrs. Arbuthnot, the Foreign Minister naturally defended his wife, saying 'she was incapable of doing anything unkind or tending to injure the character of anyone, but that Lady Conyngham had fancied that, because the King chose to proclaim her as his mistress, all the Ministers' wives and adherents were to pay her court, and that she had not paid that attention to Lady Castlereagh which every other woman did, of leaving her name at the door and that consequently she had not deemed it necessary to seek her out.' Castlereagh added that his wife was 'much too high-minded to pay court to *anyone*, much less to a woman whose only notoriety arose from so shameful a cause.' A little later he told Mrs. Arbuthnot that Emily 'had no ill will to Lady

Conyngham, that she had always been in the habit of inviting her occasionally to her house, but that she had never been intimate with her; and that Lady Conyngham had this year not paid her the attention of calling on her, which is the etiquette for the person last coming to London always to do; that she had certainly not felt that Lady Conyngham's new post as King's mistress gave her any additional claims, but that she should be very sorry to be a source of embarrassment to the Government and that if Lady Conyngham, on coming to London, called on her she would ask her again as she had done before.' But Lady Conyngham did not respond to this hint.

The King not unnaturally was annoyed over a situation of which his mistress made the most. In the Duke of Wellington's hearing His Majesty 'abused Lady Castlereagh violently because she took no notice of Lady Conyngham, and said it was of a piece with the treatment he uniformly met with from his Ministers'. He also blamed his Foreign Minister for bungling the business of his divorce, since the Bill of Pains and Penalties had had to be dropped owing to the danger of its being rejected by the Commons after just managing to scrape through the Upper House. At the time of the Coronation in 1821, His Majesty no longer spoke to Castlereagh, even on matters of state. On the royal visit to Ireland, which took place shortly afterwards and on which Castlereagh accompanied the Sovereign, His Majesty treated Castlereagh with marked coldness and flatly refused to have his wife in the party, although Lady Conyngham was much in evidence.

Lady Castlereagh was likewise excluded from the trip which the monarch and his Foreign Minister made shortly afterwards to Hanover, for George IV had also inherited this German kingdom from his father. The King was still on poor terms with the Foreign Secretary at the start of the visit. He did not even invite him to stay in the royal palace of Herrenhausen, so that Castlereagh and Clanwilliam, the Under-Secretary, who came too, had to put up with inferior accommodation in a damp and previously untenanted house, where they both caught bad colds. In other respects, however, the excursion was most satisfactory for the Foreign Minister. He had suggested to the King that it would be a convenient opportunity for His Majesty to meet Prince Metternich, and George IV, who was a great admirer of the Austrian Chancellor, enthusiastically agreed. Metternich gladly came to Hanover, also the two Lievens—Castlereagh made a point of including the Russian Ambassador's wife in the invitation, as he was anxious to have Metternich in a good humour. The meeting was a great success; Metternich and his mistress set about rehabilitating Castlereagh's fortunes with his royal master. They succeeded completely. Castlereagh not only regained all his former favour, but the King even spoke of dismissing Liverpool and reconstituting the Government under Castlereagh's Premiership. In fact, His Majesty made overtures in this sense to Castlereagh, which the latter declined out of loyalty to Liverpool. However, Castlereagh promised to persuade Liverpool to give Lady Conyngham's son a political appointment at Court, which the Prime Minister had hitherto refused to do, and the King and his Foreign Secretary consequently parted the best of friends. The King promised to pay a return visit to Metternich in Vienna the following year, and the others all agreed to join in the reunion as well.

No wonder the Foreign Minister was delighted with the Russian Princess. 'You cannot imagine how pleased Lord Castlereagh was to see me again,' she wrote to Metternich on 30th November 1821, the first time he called on her after his return to London from Hanover. 'He came in with open arms; I simply had to open mine half-way, so that we gave each other a kind of semi-tender embrace.'

The Austrian Chancellor had advised his mistress to make a point of cultivating the British Foreign Secretary, whose conversation, Metternich told her, she would find stimulating and amusing. Castlereagh on his side found himself greatly attracted and in his loneliness and isolation began to unburden himself of his troubles to her when they met. He would purposely waylay her at parties and receptions and whenever he caught sight of her as he was riding in the Park, he would dismount and talk to her. The King thought that they must be having an affair, and he made some pointed allusions to this possibility in the Princess's hearing. There was no foundation for this belief. Nevertheless the Russian took care to reassure her lover in Vienna that there was nothing in it. 'If you hear any remarks about my intimacy with him,' she wrote to Metternich, 'please do not think there is any harm in it. When he meets me, he fastens on to me; we spend whole evenings together and he never leaves me. The reason is quite simple. He knows very few people in society, which consists mostly of members of the other camp and of women who do not know him well enough to find him amusing. I, personally, am more civil and welcome him. It is strange how timid he is in society, as if he were just beginning. But with me it is not merely politeness; I find him thoroughly entertaining, and I owe it to you. You gave me a taste for his conversation.'

Castlereagh, as we have seen, habitually spoke in French to members of the diplomatic corps, and to Princess Lieven his bizarre expressions in that language were a constant source of amusement. 'It is extraordinary now much at ease I feel when I can talk to Prince Metternich,' he said to her. 'It is the same with you. My ideas are all fluid.' The word he used for 'fluid' was '*liquide*', which the Princess told him she found charming and would pass it on to her lover. At this he gave a loud 'Ha, ha!' On another occasion, when talking to her of the harmony which prevailed amongst the Great Powers, he said: '*Les Cabinets alliés sont tous dans un potage.*' ('I thought how you would have laughed,' she wrote to Metternich, 'and thinking of your face set me off too.')

In spite of the improvement in Castlereagh's personal relations with the King and his success with Liverpool in arranging for the Court appointment of Lady Conyngham's son, the quarrel between the two women remained as bitter as ever. To some extent, at least, the fault seemed to have lain with Lady Conyngham, who refused to take the opportunity which had been provided for her of calling on Lady Castlereagh. At the end of January 1822 Princess Lieven wrote: 'I see no means of bringing about a reconciliation with Lady Londonderry. There is the bitterest prejudice against her, though her husband is regarded with affection.' The King, who was suffering from a severe and prolonged attack of gout, became annoyed; he spoke of crying off his visit to Vienna, and the Foreign Minister grew more and more worried that he would again fall out of favour. Things continued in this unsatisfactory manner until finally they came to a head in May with a dramatic incident in which both the Ambassadress and the Minister were involved.

The Crown Princess of Denmark came to England with her husband on a visit, and the King proposed to give a dinner in her honour. In making up the list of guests, His Majesty naturally included the Foreign Secretary and his wife. When she saw this, Lady Conyngham said that if her enemy intended to be present she would not come. The King, on his side, declared that in this case he would not give the dinner. In the end he agreed to the exclusion of both the Castlereaghs, but at the same time he asked Princess Lieven to see the favourite and endeavour to persuade her to relent. The Russian thereupon called on Lady Conyngham and exerted all her powers of persuasion. She pointed out that a dinner given by the King to visiting royalty to which the diplomatic corps were invited but from which the Foreign Minister was excluded, would be in the worst possible taste, and that not to invite his wife would be a personal insult to the Minister. She also urged that the credit would belong to Lady Conyngham, and she ended by begging her as a personal favour to allow both Castlereagh and his wife to be asked. At first the King's mistress would promise nothing, but after a week of continuous entreaties on the part of Princess Lieven, during which the dinner was cancelled and re-ordered three times, Lady Conyngham eventually agreed.

The dinner duly took place. As he was entering the dining-room with his wife, Castlereagh happened to see Princess Lieven. He went up to her and asked her how the miracle had been accomplished. Before the Russian had time to reply, they were interrupted. But they met again at a reception on the following day and Castlereagh repeated his question. Princess Lieven told him, but did not emphasise her part in the arrangement. To her surprise, he spoke with unaccustomed anger.

"You have shown me my position—our position—clearly," he said. "Things cannot go on like this. We cannot put up with a Lady Conyngham who is powerful enough to offer us such affronts."

Princess Lieven replied that Lady Conyngham could not be opposed, and that consequently one had to put up with the inconveniences. Anyhow, she went on, he and Lady Castlereagh had got what they wanted over the invitation, and nobody else was any the wiser. She was telling him this, she added, by way of giving him a personal proof of her trust in him.

But the Minister refused to be pacified. "From now on I

shall be nothing more than His Majesty's very humble servant," he remarked. "We shall see how long these relations will last. If they do not last, I shall resign. I have done enough for my country and for my master. . . . Nothing can stop me."

Princess Lieven could only reiterate her surprise that he was prepared—for the sake of a women's quarrel—to sacrifice his whole career, not to mention all the political good he had done and might still do.

"I cannot sacrifice my honour and my pride," Castlereagh went on; "both are more wounded than I can say. I repeat, things cannot remain as they are." As for the King's projected journey to Vienna, His Majesty had Liverpool. Let him arrange it with him. "Let him give orders to Wellington or whoever he pleases. I can no longer receive them if he thinks I can accept, through the patronage of a foreigner, an act of politeness to which my position itself entitles me."

Princess Lieven was struck by the Minister's strange appearance. He began to talk wildly and she could not follow what he was driving at. He mentioned the Duke's name several times and seemed to think he was intriguing against him in the Cabinet. Then, suddenly turning towards Princess Lieven and looking her full in the face, he exclaimed, "And you—you are also a traitor!"

The Princess was so amazed by this outburst that she could not reply. Her eyes filled with tears and she left the reception without saying another word. Her husband followed her, and as they were getting into their carriage she told him what had passed between her and the Foreign Minister. "Well," was the Ambassador's comment, "either I am mad or he is."

Next day, Castlereagh's brother, Stewart, who was home on leave from his post in Vienna, called at the Russian Embassy and asked to see 'Madame l'Ambassadrice'. He was shown into the drawing-room. He looked puzzled and upset.

"My God, what have you done?" he asked, as soon as she came in. "My brother is in a tremendous state of agitation. On his way back from the King's dinner he came to see me and spent the whole night talking. He is humiliated to the last degree that he should owe his wife's invitation to a foreign ambassadress. He says that he can no longer remain one of His Majesty's Ministers with any self-respect. Far from bearing you any goodwill for what you have done, he is suspicious of you. He thinks you are trying to goad him into resigning his office, and that you wish it to be given to the Duke of Wellington . . . He says that you have been preparing the way for this change behind his back, that it is you who have got the Duke into the King's good graces; that you know the Duke is not my brother's friend, and that he covets my brother's office; that it is you who have gained by the quarrel between his wife and Lady Conyngham, taking all the credit for the peace which has been patched up."

The Princess had no difficulty in showing her caller how absurd and ill-founded these suspicions were. "Whatever influence I possess," she said, "I have used actively and loyally in the service of Lord Londonderry. He has had more than one proof of it. I have the most sincere regard for him. But I have also enough common sense to know that any foreigner who gets mixed up with political intrigues in England will undoubtedly end with a broken neck." She did admit, however, that she had advanced the Duke's cause with the King, though not for the purpose which the Foreign Secretary seemed to imagine. "As for the Duke's feelings for him," she remarked, "Lord Londonderry explains them strangely. He has not perhaps a more sincere friend than the Duke."

Stewart, who seemed convinced by these arguments, now went on to tell Princess Lieven that he was very worried about his brother's health. Castlereagh was quite obsessed with this idea about the Duke, he said; also, his wife was continually inciting him against Lady Conyngham, and their nights were spent bickering; and between this unhappy domestic discord and the fatigues of the House of Commons, his nerves were shattered and Stewart was afraid that his mind might possibly give way beneath the burden of his worries. Stewart added that he hardly recognised his brother for the same person and that he frequently saw him weep. At this moment, Stewart burst into tears himself.

The next time she saw the Foreign Minister, which was a few days later, she was appalled at the change which had taken place in his appearance. 'Londonderry looks ghastly,' she noted on 10th June 1822. 'He has aged five years in a week; one can see that he is a broken man ... Why on earth has Londonderry contracted these suspicions? It seems to me that I have an honest face. Why cannot he see what is in my heart?'

In spite of the scene he had made with her, and which she thought he quickly forgot, Princess Lieven and the Minister continued to meet, usually in Kensington Gardens, where Castlereagh would stroll and talk to her before going down to the House. 'His manner with me was extraordinary,' she recalled afterwards. 'His face lit up when he caught sight of me. I felt that he grew gentler with me, and he often told me so. Then he would allow himself to make the most intimate confidences. If I said a word to calm him about his ideas on his position—for it was always about his position that he spoke—he flew into a rage; and from that moment his tone would be bitter and ironical. We usually parted on less friendly terms that we met.' He became a kind of torment to her, but she felt drawn towards him, though rather frightened when he grew angry. She was convinced, however, that he felt a real friendship for her. More than once he said, 'Heavens, if only I could see you every day!'

On one of these walks the unhappy man suddenly looked

at his companion with a haggard expression and asked, "Good God, can I trust you?"

This question annoyed Princess Lieven. "Look full in my face," she said, turning to him. "What do you see there?"

Castlereagh answered with a mocking smile. "A charming face, a clever face."

Princess Lieven flushed scarlet. "No, my lord," she said. "None of that, but an honest face."

The Foreign Secretary dropped his eyes and did not say a word.

On another occasion they were discussing her plans for the summer, and Princess Lieven happened to mention the Minister's Continental journey, which had been arranged to begin in August.

"In August," Castlereagh remarked sadly, "I shall no longer be the King's Minister."

4

If Princess Lieven was the first person to detect signs of acute mental strain in the Foreign Minister, it was to another woman, Mrs. Arbuthnot, as we have seen, that Castlereagh unburdened himself in the last days of his life. What was the nature and course of his relations with this woman, whose grief at his death was so pronounced and who would never hear a word against him? She was prepared to admit that on occasion he was an indifferent speaker. But otherwise he was perfection in her eyes.

Mrs. Arbuthnot's father was the Hon. Henry Fane, a Tory M.P., and her grandfather was the 8th Earl of Westmorland. At the time of her marriage in 1815 to another Tory M.P., the Rt. Hon. Charles Arbuthnot, she was nineteen, while her husband, whose second wife she was, was twenty-six years her senior. However, their marriage was an ideally happy one, destined to be broken only by her sudden death from cholera twelve years after Castlereagh's. Her great passion was politics, and she was able to indulge it to the full by reason of her husband's position in the Government. As Chief Government Whip and Patronage Secretary, Charles Arbuthnot was Castlereagh's closest associate in the House of Commons, and it was inevitable that this connection should have brought the Leader of the House, which Castlereagh was, as well as Foreign Secretary, into frequent contact with his wife. Harriet Arbuthnot was a cultivated and intelligent woman, devoted to her husband and disapproving of the loose morals of the Prince Regent and his Court. Her friendship with Castlereagh was strictly platonic, as also were her relations with the Duke of Wellington, and it greatly upset her when it was suggested that she was the Duke's mistress. All this is evident from the private diary which she kept and which she guarded most jealously, refusing to let even such an intimate friend as Castlereagh look at it.

'I saw Lord Londonderry this morning,' she wrote in it on 7th February 1822, '. . . he is so calm-minded that he is never alarmed by anything . . . He talked to me about this Journal that I keep and was very anxious to see it, which I would not let him do.* He said he was afraid of a person who kept a journal and said that if I put into it everything I heard, it must be a most important document. He was very anxious to know if it *treated of politics*, or only where I dined, etc. I told him as little about it as I could, but I said I was very sorry I had not kept a journal all the eight years I have been living in the vortex of politics, and that it was very

*The interesting diary, which covers the years 1820 to 1832, has recently been published by Macmillan, under the editorship of Mr. Francis Bamford and the Duke of Wellington, as *The Journal of Mrs. Arbuthnot*, 2 vols. London, 1950.

unfortunate that those who, from their position, were most capable of keeping journals were exactly the persons who had not time to do so; that I could not conceive anything more interesting and important than a journal kept by him. He said it was very true, that he had often thought, if he was out of office and had a few months' leisure in the country, that he would arrange his papers and make a sort of history of his own public life, for it so happened that from the commencement of his political career he has always filled the office which was the most important one in the Government. He was Secretary in Ireland during the Irish Rebellion and carried the Union; he was Secretary of the War Department the first years of the war in Spain, and he has been at the Foreign Office during all the years when our diplomatic transactions have been of such immense importance.' Castlereagh told Mrs. Arbuthnot on this occasion that one of the most important papers he had was a letter written to him by the late King George III from Windsor Castle acquiescing ('the word he always used when an arrangement displeased him') in the Cabinet's decision to appoint Sir Arthur Wellesley to the command of the British forces in the Peninsula, but making it clear that should further reinforcements be sent out, 'a more experienced General' should supersede Wellesley. 'This happened shortly before the King's illness,' noted Mrs. Arbuthnot, 'and, had he continued at the head of affairs, Sir Arthur might never have become Duke of Wellington and we might never have had so much glory to boast of.'*

*The original of this letter, dated 27th March 1809 at Windsor Castle and signed in an almost illegible scrawl by George III, is preserved among the *Castlereagh Papers* at Mount Stewart, Co. Down. 'In agreeing to so young a Lieutenant-General holding so distinguished a command,' wrote the King, 'His Majesty must desire Lord Castlereagh will keep in view that, if the Corps in Portugal should be further increased hereafter, the claims of senior officers cannot with justice be set aside.'

With both Arbuthnot and his wife Castlereagh was thus on the most intimate terms. They constantly dined in each other's houses in London and also paid each other visits in the country, so that Mrs. Arbuthnot's recollections of the Foreign Minister are of particular value, prejudiced in his favour as she was. On 26th March 1821 she wrote in her journal: 'Walked with Lord Castlereagh and Mr. Arbuthnot to Chantrey's to see a bust which Chantrey is making of Lord Castlereagh. It was not quite finished, but it will be wonderfully like and has just the beautiful expression of his countenance when he speaks.' She was particularly struck by his appearance at King George IV's Coronation and pleased at the good reception he got from the crowd, which had jeered him only a short time previously on account of his part in the royal divorce proceedings. On this occasion Castlereagh walked alone in the procession as the only Knight of the Garter who was not a member of the House of Lords, on his way through Old Palace Yard (where the Arbuthnots were in one of the stands) from Westminster Hall to the Abbey. 'His dress was beautiful, his hat bound round with the most splendid diamonds and he looked handsomer than I ever saw him,' noted Mrs. Arbuthnot; 'the people echoed his name from one to the other the whole length of the platform and received him with repeated cheers. It was unanimously voted that he was the handsomest man in the procession. It is very strange and only shows what an extraordinary people this is, for there is certainly no reason just now why he, who a few months ago was hissed and hooted through the streets, should now be received with such acclamations.' He jokingly told Mrs. Arbuthnot afterwards that he attributed this 'popular applause' to his 'personal beauty'.

But this characteristic was no joke, as we know from Lawrence's portraits and Chantrey's bust as well as Mrs. Arbuthnot's observation. 'He was above six feet high and had a remarkably fine commanding figure, very fine dark eyes, rather a high nose and a mouth whose smile was sweeter than it is possible to describe. It was impossible to look at him and see the benevolent and amiable expression of his countenance without a disposition to like him, and over his whole person was spread an air of dignity and nobleness such as I have never seen in any other person. His manners were perfect as those of a high-born polished gentleman, and nothing could be more graceful and easy than his reception of people who attended the assemblies constantly given by Lady Londonderry.' That his wife's occasional complaints about his behaviour were unjustified Mrs. Arbuthnot was also careful to note. 'He was excessively agreeable, a great favourite amongst women and used occasionally to excite Lady Londonderry's jealousy; but he was the kindest and most affectionate of husbands, paid her the greatest possible attention and had unbounded confidence in her.'

Unlike Princess Lieven, Mrs. Arbuthnot does not seem to have noticed that there was anything the matter with Castlereagh, not even during the week or so before his death, when she saw him on several occasions—at least there is no hint of it in her journal. Only once did he complain to her about being overworked, and that was rather more than a year previously, when protracted talks were taking place on the subject of Canning's readmission to the Cabinet. Canning had resigned because he was a friend of the Queen and disagreed with the policy of the divorce proceedings, and now that the divorce had been dropped he was anxious to be a member of the Government again. On Castlereagh's fifty-second birthday (18th June 1821), Mrs. Arbuthnot wrote in her journal: 'Lord Londonderry called on me. He seems quite tired of all this discussion about Mr. Canning and the changes in the Cabinet, told me he wished he could slip his neck out of the collar and have done with the whole thing. He said he wondered Mr. Arbuthnot was alive, he had so much to do, but that they should not be able to go on without him.'

Although he and Canning had once fought a duel with pistols in the dawn of an autumn morning on Putney Heath, Castlereagh had long since ceased to bear any ill feelings towards his most prominent political rival, if indeed he ever harboured more than a momentary grievance. When Liverpool became Prime Minister after Spencer Perceval's assassination in 1812, he wished to reconstruct his Government and to let Canning return to his old post as Foreign Secretary, which he had been obliged to quit after the duel. Castlereagh, who had been given the Foreign Office by Perceval, was now quite willing to surrender it to Canning, provided he could retain the leadership of the House of Commons. But Canning had refused this generous offer in the belief that the new Government would break up soon and that he could then come in on his own terms. Four years later, in a somewhat chastened mood, he had been content to re-enter it in a less important post, only to leave it again in 1820 in the circumstances already described. Mrs. Arbuthnot, whose view of Canning's character was far from flattering, did not hesitate to tell Castlereagh what she thought about him. 'Many a dispute have we had together,' she recalled afterwards, 'when I have reproached him for his willingness to be again united in public with one who had endeavoured to undermine him with the meanest hypocrisy, who had always caused dissensions and jealousies in the Cabinet and who had finally quitted it in the most unhandsome manner and at a moment when his secession might have been to them a source of serious embarrassment.' However, Castlereagh could afford to be magnanimous. He used to tell Mrs. Arbuthnot that 'with regard to himself he had had his struggle with Canning and had left him far behind, and that therefore he had no jealousy about him

and that he thought his talents would be useful to the public.'
Castlereagh, according to Mrs. Arbuthnot, 'did not think
Canning an upright honourable man, but still he thought
he might be made a useful person.'

Canning did not after all re-enter the Cabinet in 1821,
because the King, who was still smarting from his action
over the divorce, objected. Indeed Canning had such little
hopes of ever again becoming one of the King's Ministers
that he accepted the post of Governor-General of Bengal
and was about to embark for this domain when he heard
the news of the catastrophe at Cray. Then he was to have
his chance again and to resume the same seals of office which
he had relinquished thirteen years previously. Castlereagh's
widow and family connections were indignant at this disposal of his office and felt it was an insult to his memory.
'However, I suppose it could not be helped,' noted Mrs.
Arbuthnot, 'and that it is true what the Duke says—that
could Lord Londonderry (who was always anxious for the
readmission of Canning into the Cabinet) look out of his
grave, he would approve the appointment.'

Nevertheless, she could not contemplate 'without feelings
of the utmost bitterness' that his place at the Foreign Office
should be so unworthily filled. She pressed her husband to
throw up his own post, since she felt that 'to continue with
Mr. Canning is an infidelity to the friend I so dearly loved'.
She could not bear the idea of continuing to live in the
Treasury, which was opposite the office in Downing Street
'where he no longer presides'. Nor could she abide the sight
of the familiar building in St. James's Square. 'The very
house is become odious to me in which I used so constantly
to see him,' she noted, 'and where the place he always
occupied on the sofa will incessantly remind me of the
happy hours I spent with him and which will never return.'

In an attempt to banish him from her thoughts, she buried
herself at her husband's farm in Northamptonshire. But she

could not forget him. Indeed she came upon a print of him there, 'a striking likeness', engraved from one of Lawrence's portraits. 'I confess with shame that I have spent hours in mourning over that shining countenance,' she confided in her journal, 'the image of what he was in his hours of relaxation and happiness.'

CHAPTER FOUR

Royal Relations

I

'MARRIED LUFF NEVER LASTS,' a German Princess once confided in a thick native accent to her English lady-in-waiting. 'Dat is not in de nature.' The Princess was Amelia Elizabeth Caroline, Princess of Brunswick-Wolfenbüttel, and the occasion was her first visit to England in 1795 for the purpose of marrying the Prince of Wales, later King George IV. Alas, for poor, playful Caroline, married love not only did not last, but it never really began. Her future husband was already secretly married to one woman, Mrs. Fitzherbert, and at this date was under the dominant influence of another, his mistress, Lady Jersey. Indeed the marriage was largely promoted by Lady Jersey, who did not wish to see her own charms displaced. But it was destined to end disastrously for all parties. A marriage can survive and even thrive where the wife chooses the mistress, but no union has ever been known to succeed where the mistress has chosen the wife. So it was with 'Prinney' and Princess Caroline. As soon as he first set eyes on her, the Prince realised his mistake. On their wedding-night he arrived in the nuptial chamber dead drunk and his bride, with whose supper Lady Jersey had considerately mixed some Epsom salts, let him sleep it off near the fire-place.

Exactly nine months and a day later the Princess had borne her husband a daughter, called Charlotte, who was thus in the direct line of succession to the throne. Caroline's labour had been long and difficult, and thereafter 'Prinney' let it be known that he did not expect her to become a mother again. 'Our inclinations are not in our power,' he remarked, 'nor should either of us be held answerable to the other, because nature has not made us suitable to each other.' At the same time the Prince of Wales expressed the hope that 'the rest of our lives will be passed in uninterrupted tranquillity.' That this did not and, in the nature of things, could not be, was among others to involve Castlereagh deeply and was to be a constant cause of worry and anxiety to the King's Minister for most of the last years of his life.

Caroline, it must be admitted, was a lady of robust instincts. She gave proof of them on the way over to England on the boat when she spent the night alone on deck with the first mate. When apprised of her royal master's amorous propensities, she had not hesitated to tell Lady Jersey about a love affair of her own. Though warned that such conduct was a capital offence under English law both in herself and her lover, soon she was openly boasting of her taste in 'bedfellows'. A little later she appeared with an 'adopted' son of a sailmaker called William Austin, or 'Willikins', who was widely said to be her own. 'Prove it and he shall be your King!' was her customary gleeful rejoinder to this charge. In 1806 Commissioners had been appointed to carry out a 'delicate investigation' of her conduct. They acquitted her of having an illegitimate child, but censured her levity and found her guilty of 'unworthy indiscretions'. With the end of the long war with Napoleon and the reopening of the Continent to English travellers, she departed for abroad with a circus-like entourage whose members, mostly Italian, occupied an old mail coach. Chief of her retainers was her courier, named Bartolomeo Bergami, who dressed himself up as a Hussar and was styled Baron. She caressed him in public, and he was generally believed to be her lover. After a fantastic progress round Europe by coach and the

95

Mediterranean by yacht, she eventually established her royal residence with Signor Bergami in the Villa d'Este on the shores of Lake Como. 'What a heroine in history she would have been had she behaved properly,' wrote her lady-in-waiting at this time. 'There had been something so grand in her conduct up to that period, something so magnanimous in her silent endurance of her husband's malevolence, that could not fail to create a strong feeling in her favour. But when she went abroad, she dropped the grand historical character of an injured Queen and became a Mrs. Thompson parted from Mr. Thompson and going in search of amusement.'

Her husband, now Prince Regent, not unnaturally wished to break the legal bonds which tied him to this woman, whom he had last seen ten years previously. He therefore despatched a special commission to Italy, the so-called Milan Commission, to collect evidence of his wife's infidelity, on which he hoped to found divorce proceedings. This action he took on his own initiative and the Government had no responsibility for it. But its members were naturally aware of what was happening and furthermore Castlereagh's assistance as Foreign Minister was directly sought by the Regent. Thus, under the strictest pledge of secrecy, Castlereagh instructed his brother Stewart, then Ambassador in Vienna, to enlist the support of the Austrian Government in the inquiries, since at that period Northern Italy formed part of the Imperial dominions.

At the beginning of 1816 Castlereagh began the detailed, secret correspondence with his brother which was eventually to lead to the Bill of Pains and Penalties. Stewart was first warned of the importance of 'not risking an exposure except on *sure* grounds' on the part of the agents he employed, who 'ought to secure the presence of some unexceptionable evidences who could testify that they had *ocular demonstration* of the Princess's frailties'.

'English witnesses are to be preferred,' Castlereagh went on; 'and should such an attempt be made, it is material (lest it should fail) that it should be so made as not to implicate you or any other person in the Prince Regent's service. You will keep in mind that there are two objects to be aimed at. The first and best would be such unqualified proof of what no person can morally doubt as would for ever deliver the Prince Regent from the scandal of having a woman so lost to all decency in the relation of his wife. To effect this, or to justify in prudence a proceeding for divorce, the proofs must be direct and unequivocal, and the evidence such with respect to the parties to be examined as would preclude their testimony from being run down and discredited. We must always recollect that this proceeding, if to be taken, must ultimately be a parliamentary one. Party would then soon give it the character of a question not merely between the Prince and Princess, but between the Prince and Princess Charlotte, and a great deal of factious intrigue and unpleasantness might grow out of such a case, especially if there was any disrepute which could be thrown upon the proofs, or if the evidence was merely circumstantial and not direct. But there is another most important object short of divorce, viz. to accumulate such a body of evidence* as may at any time enable the Prince Regent to justify himself for refusing to receive the Princess in this country or to admit her to the enjoyment of any of those honorary distinctions, to which his wife, if received into his Court and family, would be entitled.'

*Much of the information thus collected found its way into the old State Paper Office and thence into the Public Record Office. In 1933 two bundles of documents concerning Caroline were transferred from the Public Record Office to the Royal Archives at Windsor, 'where they now remain and where, it is understood, they are not open to inspection'. See replies from the Financial Secretary to the Treasury to my questions in the House of Commons, 2nd February 1956: *Parliamentary Report*, cols. 1083-84.

During the next two years the evidence thus asked for was assiduously collected by secret service agents, the documentary proofs were neatly deposited in a green bag, and the witnesses were asked to hold themselves in readiness if called upon. Meanwhile the Princess would occasionally emerge from the Villa d'Este and resume her travels, to the embarrassment of British diplomatic representatives into whose territories she ventured, not to mention other local notabilities, who were sometimes uncertain how to treat her. 'She principally complains that the assurances she alleges were given her before she left England have been broken,' wrote Castlereagh in May 1817, 'of being everywhere received as the Princess of Wales. I expect her suite, after robbing her, will in some of her pilgrimages put her to death. She must be deranged—vice and folly would not explain her proceedings.' In the same month she tried to see the Austrian Emperor, but he refused to receive her, on his Chancellor Metternich's advice, for which action the Prince Regent assured him that his gratitude would last to the tomb. She spoke of returning to England in search of what she called justice for herself, and in 1819 applied for and obtained from the Civil Governor of Milan a passport in the name of her lady-in-waiting, Countess Oldi. On this occasion she got as far as Lyons, where she met her legal adviser, the Whig Mr. Henry Brougham, who told her that the Cabinet had agreed with her husband that no divorce proceedings would be begun so long as she remained abroad, but that proceedings would be instituted as soon as she crossed the Channel. This piece of news caused her to change her plans and she withdrew instead to the south of France. 'I have always doubted of her real purpose to come to this country,' noted Castlereagh on 9th November 1819. 'She is fully aware of the disgust which is universally felt on her subject and that by all the higher ranks she would be shunned. She may bully and threaten, but I doubt her having the courage either to emancipate herself from Bergami or *voluntarily* to encounter the public contempt, which Her Royal Highness would inevitably experience from all respectable persons.'

The Princess did not remain quiescent for long. Early in 1820 the mad old King George III died, and his obese and gouty son at last came into his royal inheritance. The new sovereign's change of status inevitably produced fresh complications in his relations with his wife. He now demanded his divorce and, as a first step, insisted that Caroline's name should be excluded from the Liturgy—indeed he had long been of the opinion that she was past praying for. For her part, she wrote to Liverpool and Castlereagh, demanding that her name be inserted in the Prayer Book and also that orders be given to all British Ambassadors, Ministers and Consuls that she should be acknowledged and received as Queen of England. 'After the speech made by Lord Castlereagh in the House of Commons in answer to Mr. Brougham,' she declared, 'I do not expect to receive further insults. I have also demanded that a palace should be prepared for my reception—England is my real home to which I shall immediately fly.' At the same time she wrote to Brougham, inviting him to meet her at Geneva. Had he been able to do so, he could no doubt have persuaded her to return to Italy, since the Government was willing to increase her allowance on condition that she kept out of England. Unfortunately Brougham did not wish to go so far away from Westminster, but he agreed to cross the Channel and meet her near the French coast. Meanwhile a Radical alderman of the City of London, named Wood, succeeded in getting hold of her, and Brougham could do nothing when he eventually saw her in St. Omer.

On the morning of the 6th June 1820, Queen Caroline crossed in the packet to Dover, and to her agreeable surprise was greeted by a salute of guns appropriate to a crowned head. She received an enthusiastic welcome on her journey to London, although the crowd when she arrived at the outskirts of the metropolis was not as great as was expected owing to the lateness of the hour. From Greenwich she rode in an open landau, with the Radical alderman by her side. Castlereagh happened to be with the King in Carlton House when the cavalcade passed, and was shocked by Wood's vulgarity in occupying such a conspicuous place of honour. 'When opposite the Palace, this innocent citizen stood up without his hat in the landau, and invoked a cheer from the shabby crew that attended the party.' Caroline, on the other hand, stopped the procession and, waving her fair hand, cried 'Long Live the King'. Later that night, after he had returned to St. James's Square, Castlereagh wrote to his brother in Vienna an account of what had happened: 'The die is cast. The Queen is at Alderman Wood's in South Audley Street, and the green bag with all the papers on the table of both Houses. We shall name our committee to take them into consideration, and to advise the House whether any and what proceedings should be had thereupon to-morrow. So as now the whole proofs must be adduced . . . send us all the witnesses. We shall have a difficult and tedious proceeding; but we have so managed as to place the King on strong ground.'

2

Not unnaturally the Queen became the rallying point for all the popular elements in the country. Throughout the night of her arrival and for many days and nights afterwards, the London mob streamed through the streets shouting 'Long live the Queen!' and making passers-by do likewise. Castlereagh's windows in St. James's Square were repeated-ly broken, so were those of his aunt, the King's ex-mistress

Lady Hertford, although curiously enough no assault was made on those of the reigning favourite, Lady Conyngham. Five days after the Queen's first appearance Princess Lieven went to a soirée in St. James's Square. 'The evening at Lady Castlereagh's was very agitated,' she wrote in her diary. 'The Ministers had just had an expected Cabinet meeting, which produced much chatter and comment . . . We live here in continual tumult and anxiety. There is something happening every hour. This tension wears one out mentally and physically; I believe that the Queen will age us all.'

Castlereagh, on whose shoulders fell all the odium for the treatment of Queen Caroline, was hooted and hissed whenever he was recognised. Eventually, as we have seen, when Her Majesty established herself a few doors away in St. James's Square, he found her presence too embarrassing for comfort. 'The Queen's coming to so bad a house, when the Board of Works conveyed her a list of several better to choose from,' he told his brother at the time, 'clearly proved either that she wished to point me out as a victim to her rabble or that she meant to bring on a conflict and to give me a share of the honour. I have disappointed her on both projects without any personal inconvenience by simply moving a bed to the Office, shutting up my windows and removing my plate and papers from the house.' For safety he sent his wife down to Cray.

However, Castlereagh's spirits kept up, and he wrote hopefully to Metternich, who had been very helpful over the witnesses. 'It is something to have done our best to avoid an evil and to have no other course left but to brave it. I doubt not we shall carry the King through his difficulties. The public mind is still much poisoned, but truth never fails in this country finally to triumph.' For a month one of the green bags lay unopened on the table of the House of Commons, while negotiations took place with the Queen. The basis of the negotiations conducted by Castlereagh and

Wellington with Brougham and Denman, the Queen's legal advisers, were that, while the King retracted nothing and she admitted nothing, an annuity of £50,000 a year would be settled on her on condition that she resumed her Continental residence. The negotiations came to nothing because the King insisted that her name should be omitted from the Liturgy ('You might as easily move Carlton House,' said Castlereagh), while his estranged wife, who wished to be prayed for in the churches, refused to accept any terms in which this point was not conceded. Meanwhile, the other green bag had been opened in the House of Lords and its contents examined by a Secret Committee. Early in July this body reported that 'the evidence affecting the honour of the Queen was such as to require, for the dignity of the Crown and the moral feeling and honour of the country, a solemn inquiry'. The Cabinet, with the King's consent, arranged for the preparation of a Bill of Pains and Penalties, which would deprive Queen Caroline of her regal status. This measure was to be introduced in the Lords, and after its first reading, the 'inquiry'—in effect, the Queen's trial on the charge of adultery with Bartolomeo Bergami—would begin.

'Upon the whole,' wrote Castlereagh to his brother on 15th July, 'I do not think matters up to the present point could have worked more favourably. We have contrived to get on to the point of actual trial, keeping the King always on high and safe grounds. His Majesty has had all the grace of forbearance without conceding anything; and the mind of Parliament has been gradually brought to settle to the calamity of a public trial of the Queen as an inevitable evil from which no prudential effort could relieve them. This is an immense point gained. Another has been the throwing the lead in the inquiry upon the Peers . . . In this assembly the charge will be examined on oath, with gravity and decorum, so as to clear away the rubbish before we have to deal with it in the Commons.' This plan meant postponing the Coronation, a step which Princess Lieven thought was forced on the Ministers by the knowledge that the loyalty of the army was in doubt. 'I never agreed to anything so reluctantly,' Castlereagh noted, 'lest it should appear to be a concession to the Queen and her mob. But the general feeling of our best and firmest friends was against crowning a King and trying a Queen at one and the same moment. I believe it was wise, but it has sadly stuck in my stomach from the indecency at Her Majesty's conduct.' At the same time Castlereagh had to admit privately that the King's behaviour was nearly as bad. 'It is lamentable,' he told his brother, 'that our Royal Master, when a Bill of Divorce is pending, should be living publicly at the Cottage at Windsor with the Conynghams, and walking out every day with my lady. Never was such an unfortunate infatuation at his age and in his position.'

The trial was fixed to begin on 17th August. 'On that day,' Princess Lieven informed Metternich, 'the peers of the three realms have to be in Parliament at ten o'clock in the morning, under pain of imprisonment in the Tower or of a fine of 500 guineas a day. Only septuagenarians are excused, and they will be most punctual so as not to give away their age. What a trial we shall witness! Those grave spiritual lords, how will they take the pretty things they are going to hear? . . . Well, *mon Prince*, I am not sure that she will be found guilty. By the House of Lords, yes. But the Commons?' Meanwhile, the Queen announced that she would defend herself with vigour. Her plan, according to Princess Lieven, was 'to give her own account of the relations between the King and herself, to reveal everything she knows about his behaviour, and not to confine herself to that alone, but to give a little historical narrative of the behaviour of each member of the Royal Family, not forgetting the off-spring of the unmarried Princesses.' Many strange rumours were in circulation. One was that Bergami was really a woman, and that Her Majesty would produce proofs to that effect. 'You have no idea of the ridiculous stories that are put about,' Princess Lieven told her lover, 'and of the facility with which people tend to believe any story that exonerates the Queen.'

On the other hand, there was the usual crop of smoking-room witticisms. The amusing Lord Norbury, with whom Castlereagh had been closely associated in his early political career in Ireland, was responsible for two of the best of these. Asked if he knew how the Queen had amused herself in Algiers, Lord Norbury replied that she was 'as happy as the Dey is long'. To another query as to which of the newspapers Her Majesty read, the answer was that 'she took in *The Courier.*

The Bills of Pains and Penalties was introduced in the House of Lords on 19th August, and two days later the examination of witnesses began. 'I have not had the heart to read the evidence,' noted Princess Lieven on the third day; 'it is too disgusting. Is the Queen really a woman? And how can the House of Lords, uniting as it does all that is most dignified and most exalted in the greatest nation in the world, lower itself by listening to such vile trash?' Castlereagh attended the trial daily. 'Here is Castlereagh, smiling as usual, though I think awkwardly,' wrote Mr. Creevey. With the diarist he watched Her Majesty pop 'all at once' into the Lords' Chamber, looking like a Dutch toy, duck to the throne, duck to the Peers and jump into her chair. 'Her dress was black-figured gauze, with a good deal of trimming, lace, etc.,' added Creevey; 'her sleeves are perfectly episcopal; a handsome white veil, so thick as to make it very difficult for me, who was as near to her as anyone, to see her face . . . a few straggling ringlets on her neck, which I flatter myself from their appearance were not Her Majesty's own property.' Princess Lieven, who saw her at close quarters at this time, noticed 'two enormous black eyebrows' and 'the contents of two pots of rouge on her cheeks'—'she looks completely brazen'.

Unhappily for Her Majesty, the first witness for the prosecution was one of her Italian servants, by name Theodore Majocchi. The unexpected appearance of one she thought she could trust so took the Queen by surprise that, at the first sight of him, she called out 'Theodore', or, as some thought, '*Traditore*' (traitor). She thereupon rushed wildly from the Chamber. Majocchi's testimony was certainly a betrayal of his royal mistress, for he swore that while on board the yacht *Polacre* in the Mediterranean, she frequently had baths with Bergami in a tent on the deck. When in Jerusalem with her bizarre retinue she had founded a new order, the Order of Saint Caroline, with lilac ribbon and red cross, and had created Bergami hereditary Grand Master. A neat epigram, inspired by Majocchi's revelations, was soon going the rounds.

> The Grand Master of St. Caroline
> Has found promotion's path.
> He is made both (K)night Companion
> And Commander of the Bath.

The Queen, who had announced at the start that she would attend the proceedings every day so as to confound the witnesses by her presence, soon became bored. She brought a backgammon set along with her and would play in an adjoining room, with Alderman Wood. Once she fell asleep in the Lords' Chamber, an occurrence which gave rise to another epigram.

> Her conduct at present no censure affords,
> She sins not with peasants, but sleeps with the Lords.

Princess Lieven thought she was really a mental case and could not understand why her doctor was not questioned about her sanity. 'If they pronounced her mad, they would avoid all this scandal and be bearers of truth besides.' Nevertheless the populace refused to believe any evil of her, and continued to greet her with customary enthusiasm. Castlereagh grew worried as to the outcome of the business. On 1st September he wrote to his brother: 'The difficulties which we have to contend against are immense. 1st. The public prejudice, which is inconceivably strong, perhaps more against the King than for the Queen, but desperately against relieving him by divorce, whatever may be done with her. This is a very general feeling within Parliament as well as out of doors. 2ndly. The protracted nature of the proceedings with the battle likely to rage the whole time in an unbridled and, beyond all example, licentious press, with Her Majesty acting the part of chief libeller . . . 3rdly. There is a cabal of the House of Commons, and evidence at the Bar of perhaps interminable length, new points of law and grave constitutional questions starting up at every step. 4thly. There is the spirit of Party, which forgets everything in the hope of shaking the Government . . . Never was there a more embarrassing concern, but we must go straight forward and leave the rest to Providence. The King is at the Cottage, very anxious, as you may well imagine, and fully alive now to the nature of those difficulties, which I always told His Majesty would be the inevitable attendants upon this proceeding. . . .' In a moment of candour, the Foreign Minister confessed to the Russian Ambassador, who duly reported it to St. Petersburg, that, if the Government had realised what would happen, they would have done anything to avoid the scandal.

The Italian witnesses for the Crown cut sorry enough figures, and the failure of their memories under cross-examination by the Queen's Counsel soon made '*Non mi ricordo*' a popular catchword, much to Castlereagh's chagrin. After the Crown case had been closed, their lordships adjourned for three weeks, resuming in October, when both the Sovereign and his Consort suffered further humiliations. The Ministers, according to Greville, looked upon the progress of the trial in the light of a campaign, and upon each day's proceedings as a sort of battle, and by the impression made by the evidence they considered that they had gained a victory or sustained a defeat. This impression was borne out by the leading Minister himself. 'In an ordinary trial the issue is Guilty or Not Guilty,' he wrote to his brother on 7th October. 'Here it is: will you legislate or not on the case upon the conflicting testimony of contradictory evidence?' For instance, Lieutenant Hownam, a naval officer on board the *Polacre*, gave evidence for the Queen, but under cross-examination he was forced to admit that Bergami slept in her tent. In the eyes of many, this admission conclusively proved the Queen's guilt. 'The strenuous opposers of the Bill, however, by no means allow this,' noted Greville at the time, and 'make a mighty difference between sleeping dressed under a tent and being shut up at night in a room together, which the supporters of the Bill contend would have been quite or nearly the same thing.' But even the Bill's opponents, who were convinced by the unfortunate lieutenant's evidence—incidentally he added to the general impression by fainting in the Chamber—were still determined to vote against its second reading 'upon grounds of expediency'.

By every Foreign Office bag labelled for Vienna, Castlereagh sent a progress report to his brother. 'The fate of the Bill still hangs in suspense,' he wrote on 29th October, 'and, as it moves on, fresh food for inquiries seems to present future resources for opposition . . . The impression of Her Majesty's guilt is very general, but some dislike a Bill of Pains and Penalties, some think the proofs not sufficiently direct, some that the country is endangered by keeping the discussion for [such] a length of time afloat. Most of all consider that the Bill will never pass into law and that if it is to fail, it had better fail in the Lords . . . If we cannot carry the Bill, I trust we shall at least establish the guilt of the Queen in such a manner as to render her but little formidable to the King's personal comfort and position.'

The evidence on both sides being concluded, Lord Liverpool moved the second reading of the Bill on 6th November. This was carried by a majority of twenty-eight. Two days later, in committee, the divorce clause which was not pressed by the Government, passed by sixty-seven. That night Castlereagh went to the theatre, where he was promptly recognised. 'Castlereagh got roughly handled at Covent Garden last night,' wrote Mr. Creevey; 'so much so as to be obliged to decamp from the house.' The reason for the lack of enthusiasm on the part of the Ministers for the divorce clause, 'which they knew was distasteful to the people,' was noted by Princess Lieven in her diary. 'Without that clause, the Bill might pass in the Commons; with it, never,' she wrote. 'So the Ministers are now siding against the divorce; at once the Opposition insist on the divorce with the twofold aim of imperilling the Bill in the Commons and of pleasing the King. The King finds himself deserted by his Ministers and supported by the Whigs in his dearest wish—the divorce. Yesterday the majority in favour of that clause was made up by the enemies of the Government. Isn't it extraordinary? Morality and the peace of the country go for nothing: thirst for power is the only thing that counts.' No wonder the Ambassadress was disgusted by the spectacle and no longer found it amusing.

The third reading took place on 10th November and when the tellers had announced the figures it was found that the majority in favour of the Bill had fallen to nine. In these circumstances, after hastily consulting his Cabinet colleagues, the Prime Minister decided to withdraw the measure, which he did by moving in the traditional formula that it be read 'this day six months'. This was agreed to in spite of the Lord Chancellor's loud 'Not content' from the Woolsack. The Queen was waiting in an adjoining chamber. Then they brought her the news—'I am lost,' she cried, bursting into tears. 'Which convinces me,' said Princess Lieven, 'that she is a woman of intelligence.' Castlereagh explained to his brother that it was not usual to send any measure of vital importance upon a small majority from one House to the other; also that prospects of success in the Commons had grown more unpromising, 'and failure would have served to whitewash the Queen and enabled the Radicals and Opposition to press her claims to be treated as an injured and innocent person'. He went on:

In closing the proceedings in the Lords, her guilt is established upon the uncontrolled decision of the judicial branch of the Legislature—second reading carried by 28, the preamble and report without a division, and a considerable number of those approving her guilt, who nevertheless voted against the Bill—she stands thus degraded, though not punished. The diminution of numbers on the third reading was partly owing to conscientious scruples against the divorce clause, and partly to some peers wishing to establish her guilt but not to expose the country to all the evils of protracted proceedings in the House of Commons. I should have felt it my duty to fight the question to the last had the Bill come down; but there is no possibility of estimating the embarrassments in which we would have found ourselves. When we came to the examination of witnesses, we should have had no judges to guide us; all sorts of questions would have been asked and pressed; we should have had endless motions for adjournment, false evidence without end, and a cloud of witnesses to throw dirt upon the Milan Commission, against whose testimony we should be without defence, as time would not be granted to bring counter proof from Italy.

Upon the whole, under all the daily increasing difficulties, my conviction is that in going further we should have fared worse. The King was strongly impressed himself with this opinion and was against its going to the House of Commons. But, with his usual ignorance of parliamentary management and habitual disposition to get himself and Government into scrapes, he wants us now to meet Parliament on the 23rd [November] and try some new effort to get rid of the Queen. We shall, however, press a prorogation until January, and in the interim the fermentation may subside. We can judge our course better then; and if we keep quiet and make no overtures to the Queen, it is possible she may either offer terms to us or go abroad and leave her friends to act for her.

I think the King's health, as might be expected, is a little shaken. He is thin and ill at ease, complains of want of sleep, and although calm in manner can hardly sustain the miserable state of annoyance he leads. In short, my dear Charles, he now has found that I was but too true a prophet of what it is to contend with a desperate and malignant woman, in a country full of treason and a licentious press, and with a measure to carry through both Houses unparalleled in the history of the country, and in every stage of which questions spring up that shake not only the Administration but the throne itself to its foundation. . . .

Immediately afterwards Castlereagh was summoned to a meeting of the Cabinet where, according to Mrs. Arbuthnot, 'there was a terrible scene'. The Prime Minister 'was in a phrensy', and 'complained of the ill usage he had received from several in the room', particularly the Lord Chancellor whom he 'abused'. He ended by crying. It was at this meeting that the prorogation of Parliament was agreed upon. Unwillingly the King was compelled by his Minister to prorogue Parliament until the New Year. The Opposition in the Commons of course objected, and Denman was actually on his feet reading a communication from the Queen, when Black Rod appeared to summon the Members to attend their Lordships' House. As the Speaker left the Chair, followed by Castlereagh and some others from the Government Front Bench, there were shouts of 'Shame! Shame!' One Whig M.P. called out 'It is scandalous', and Mr. Creevy noted in his journal that 'certainly such a scene has never occurred in the House of Commons since Charles the 1st's time'.

Meanwhile the Queen went to St. Paul's attended by a crowd of 50,000 people to give thanks for her acquittal. A little later the King went to Drury Lane Theatre, and, with the thought of his approaching Coronation uppermost in the audience's mind, he was cheered 'as if', remarked Princess Lieven, 'he were the most virtuous, the most fatherly, the greatest of Kings'. The only discordant note came from a voice in the gallery which called out, 'Where's your wife, Georgy?' Truth to tell, the public were getting tired of Caroline; enthusiasm began to wane, particularly as people came to realise that her conduct, as revealed by the evidence of her naval officers, Lieutenants Hownam and Flynn, had not been such as they would approve in their own wives and daughters. Her stock sank lower when it was announced that she had accepted a pension from the Government, and popular feeling was now reflected in the celebrated rhyme of an anonymous pamphleteer:

> Gracious Queen, we thee implore,
>   Go away and sin no more;
> But if that effort be too great,
>   Go away at any rate.

On 13th March 1821 Castlereagh wrote to his brother: 'The Queen's question may be regarded as finally and triumphantly closed by Her Majesty's acceptance, in defiance of her own message, of the provision made by Parliament. The letter she wrote is quite her own in style, spelling, etc. and is submissive to the King. Brougham has gone the circuit, apparently broke down both in looks and spirit, as he certainly is in reputation; and the Alderman [Wood], having fixed a rendezvous with Her Majesty to prepare a proper answer to Lord Liverpool, was dismayed to learn that the Queen had answered the communication of her own hand the day before. . . . She has quarrelled with the Whigs, abused Brougham, and will soon leave the country . . .' It may be added that it was her legal champion Brougham who was responsible for the pun which made her 'pure innocence' (innosense)'

The unfortunate Caroline lingered on in England, hoping to provide some counter-attraction to the Coronation. Although no official rôle was assigned to her at this ceremony, she turned up at Westminster Abbey and as one final humiliation was refused admission by the door-keeper because she had no ticket. She retired amid the groans and cheers of the waiting crowd, and the next thing that was heard of her was three weeks later, when Castlereagh, who was with the King in Ireland, heard that she had suddenly died. 'In doing so,' noted Princess Lieven, 'she made one last difficulty for her enemies—she upset the festivities in Dublin. And in London, what are they to do with her chaste remains? That is the only embarrassment she is from now on in a position to cause them. She did her best but her death at this moment is a mere luxury, for alive she no longer inconvenienced anyone.'

There was indeed this final embarrassment. The sight of her coffin, on which at her request she was described as 'the injured Queen of England', caused a riot as it was conveyed out of Hyde Park. The escorting troops opened fire on the crowd, killing two persons and wounding several others.

4

One day during the Queen's trial, Castlereagh on coming out of the Foreign Office met his colleague, Lord Sidmouth, the former Speaker Addington, who was then Home Secretary. Sidmouth had recently had a kick on his knee from a horse, and Castlereagh gave him his arm for support as they walked to the House of Commons. They were recognised in Parliament Street, and were soon surrounded by a jeering and groaning mob. "Here we go," said the Home Secretary, "the two most popular men in England." "Yes," answered Castlereagh, "through a grateful and admiring multitude."

Although Sidmouth as Home Secretary was nominally responsible for the repressive domestic legislation passed at this time—the so-called Six Acts, which restricted the right of public meeting, authorised magistrates to search for arms and increased the penalties for publishing seditious libels— he sat in the Lords, to whose deliberations the public paid little more attention than they do today. It was on Castlereagh, who had to introduce these measures in the Commons as Leader of the House, that public odium largely fell.

He was particularly blamed in the country at large for the so-called 'Manchester Massacre', when a body of cavalry dispersed a Radical meeting in St. Peter's Fields, Manchester, with a sabre charge. We have already seen how he had to leave his house in St. James's Square, lest the mob should take it into their heads to pull down the building. His niece, Lady Brownlow, relates how one night he arrived home to find an angry mob attacking the house with bricks and paving-stones. He mingled quietly with the attackers until someone whispered, 'You are known, and had better go in.' He did so, and went up to the drawing-room on the first floor, closing the shutters of the four windows 'with the utmost composure', as a shower of stones fell around him. Next day his niece called in her father's carriage to know what had happened and found him on the point of leaving the house on foot. She persuaded him to get into the carriage, which he did, but he insisted on looking out of the window at the crowd, which had again gathered menacingly. His niece begged him 'not to let his nose be seen' for it might be recognised, and she feared for the safety of the vehicle. 'This made him laugh,' Lady Brownlow recalled afterwards, 'and he turned his head and talked with me, thus putting his face and my father's carriage out of jeopardy.'

On another occasion, about this time, Castlereagh went to the hustings in Covent Garden to speak in support of the Tory candidate. As soon as he appeared, the Radical candidate, the famous 'Orator' Hunt, said to the assembled electors, 'Allow me to present to you Viscount Castlereagh.' At this the yelling became ferocious and as he left the hustings with Lord Clanwilliam, who had accompanied him, the crowd hustled them along the street. When they reached St. Martin's Lane, their attendants became so threatening that Castlereagh and his companion were obliged to seek refuge in a shop. There being apparently no back exit and

the crowd showing no sign of dispersing, Clanwilliam somehow managed to crawl out between the legs of the besiegers,
whence he made his way to Bow Street for police aid. In due
course the reinforcements arrived and released the unfortunate Minister. They then escorted him down Whitehall,
still followed by the mob. When they reach the Admiralty,
the constables formed a line across the entrance while
Castlereagh and Clanwilliam went in. As they did so, Castlereagh turned round and, taking off his hat, bowed, and
smiling, said: 'Gentlemen, I thank you for your escort!'
He then passed through the Admiralty with Clanwilliam
and completed his walk with no further disturbance through
Green Park to St. James's Square.

It is noteworthy that he and Sidmouth were singled out
for special treatment in the plans of the so-called Cato Street
conspirators. This band of ruffians headed by a Lincolnshire
farmer's illegitimate son named Arthur Thistlewood, who
had been an ensign in the militia, devised a plot to murder
the entire Cabinet, seize some pieces of artillery which had
been left unguarded in London, set fire to the Mansion
House and other public buildings, dethrone King George
IV, and proclaim a republic. The Cabinet was to dine in a
body at Lord Harrowby's house in Grosvenor Square on
23rd February 1820, a few weeks after the King's accession.
'As there has not been a dinner for so long, there will no
doubt be fourteen or sixteen there,' confessed Thistlewood
afterwards, 'and it will be a rare haul to murder them all
together.' The conspirators arranged to meet in a loft above
a stable in Cato Street, off the Edgware Road, and thence
to proceed to Grosvenor Square, where they were to rush in
and murder the Ministers as they sat at dinner. The heads
of Castlereagh and Sidmouth were to be immediately cut off
and brought away as trophies, for which purpose bags were
prepared. Fortunately for the Cabinet and unluckily for the
conspirators, one of their number turned informer and his

information was confirmed by 'a poor man' who, according to Castlereagh's friend Croker, gave Harrowby in the Park a note addressed to Castlereagh, or as he spelled it 'Castell-ray', warning him of the danger, although the note was so badly written and spelled as to be almost unintelligible. The dinner-party was accordingly put off, and the police and a detachment of troops surprised the desperate men in Cato Street as they were about to set off for Lord Harrowby's house. In the ensuing scuffle Thistlewood and several of the others escaped, Thistlewood running a constable through the body with his sword in the attempt. Most of them were captured next day. The rest of the story was told by Castlereagh to his brother after he had spent most of the day at a meeting of the Privy Council, specially convened for the purpose of examining the conspirators.

You will be shocked at the official report of our conspiracy. There cannot exist a doubt that, had our information not been such as to enable us to watch all their movements and to interpose when we deemed fit, the 15 Cabinet Ministers would have been murdered yesterday in Harrowby's dining parlour. Thistlewood amongst this party of assassins when assembled had 14 picked men, all ripe for slaughter. They would have moved to the attack in 10 minutes had not the police arrived.

After he had escaped from the place of rendezvous, he went to Grosvenor Square with the sword in his hand bloody with which he had murdered the constable, and then went to Harrowby's door and returned, on discovering that sentinels guarded the front and rear of the house, to his place of concealment. Our information did not fail us and he was seized in his hiding place this morning in bed. The constable who first entered the room suddenly threw himself upon him, and thus fettered his exertions until he was secured. He is a most desperate dog.

Harrowby's dinner was left to wait for the arrival of the Cabinet at a late hour, so as not to arrest the preparations of the assassins. We had at one time an idea of going there to dinner and receiving their attack. But as this would have involved a point of prudence the necessity of some preparations for defence, which could not be managed without exciting observation, we thought it better to stay away from the festive board, and not to suffer it to go to single combat between Thistlewood and Marshal Liverpool.

The whole has been managed without a fault; and if you consider that we Ministers have now for months been the objects of these desperate concerts, planning our destruction, sometimes collectively, sometimes in detail, but always intent upon the object, and with our own complete knowledge, you will allow that we are tolerably cool troops, and that we have not manoeuvred armies to bring it to a final catastrophe, in which they were not only all caught in their own net, but that we can carry into a court of justice a state conspiracy, which will be proved beyond the possibility of cavil and which would form no inconsiderable feature in the *causes célebres* of treasonable and revolutionary transactions.

Thistlewood and ten of his companions were subsequently convicted of treason and condemned to death. Asked if he had anything to say why sentence should not be duly pronounced, Thistlewood began his dying speech from the dock by saying: 'This to me is a mockery—for were the reasons I could offer incontrovertible, and were they enforced upon me by the eloquence of a Cicero, still would the vengeance of my Lords Castlereagh and Sidmouth be satiated only in the purple stream which circulates through a heart more enthusiastically vibrating to every impulse of patriotism and honour than that of any of those privileged traitors to their country, who lord it over the lives and property of the sovereign people with barefaced impunity.' Another of the condemned men, named Brunt, spoke with equal conviction. 'Lords Castlereagh and Sidmouth have been the cause of the death of millions,' he declared from the dock. 'I conspired to put them out of the world, but I did not intend to commit high treason. In undertaking to kill them and their fellow ministers, I did not expect to save my own life, but I was determined to die a martyr in my country's cause and to avenge the innocent blood shed at Manchester.'

Thistlewood and four others met their fate outside Newgate on 1st May 1820. 'The conspirators, Thistlewood and Co., were hanged an hour ago,' wrote Princess Lieven to Metternich the same morning; 'and, at the moment, the streets are full of music, of drums and of people in masks. It is the festival of the chimney-sweeps, and they are dancing at every corner.' The Russian Ambassadress seems to have privately disapproved of capital punishment, for she continued: 'It makes me sad ... I feel pity for these poor human beings, for these aberrations of mind and imagination. I do not believe in the existence of a human being evil at heart; that would be to doubt the Creator. A false exaltation—such is the motive of crime. Why did Brunt die crying "Long live liberty!"? Why did that question dominate him at the moment of saying good-bye? Even in him the emotion is not criminal.' Among those who witnessed the execution was Cecil Fane, brother of Castlereagh's friend, Mrs. Arbuthnot. He had never seen a hanging before, and he went out of curiosity to a house near-by where a room had been fitted up for the convenience of spectators. But at the last moment he could not bear to witness the revolting spectacle and, according to his sister retired into a corner of the room and hid himself so that he might not see the drop fall, 'which excited great contempt in the people who were in the room with him'. Among them was one woman, young and pretty and 'very decent looking', who kept her eyes fixed on the scaffold all the time and, when the condemned men had hung for a few moments, exclaimed, 'There's two of them not dead yet!'

A few days later the Austrian Chancellor received another letter from London, which also came by diplomatic bag. It bore the British Foreign Minister's signature and was written in sterner language than that employed by Princess Lieven. 'Your Highness will observe that, although we have made an immense progress against Radicalism, the monster still lives and shows himself in new shapes,' wrote Castlereagh, 'but we do not despair of crushing him by time and perseverance. The laws have been reinforced, the juries do their duty, and wherever the mischief in its labyrinth breaks forth, it presents little real danger, while it furnishes the means of making those salutary examples which are so difficult whilst treason works in secrecy and does not disclose itself in overt acts.'

5

A fortnight after the Coronation was over, Castlereagh set out to accompany the King on his State Visit to Ireland. He went as one of the Ministers in attendance on His Majesty—the other was Lord Sidmouth—but owing to the jealousy of Lady Conyngham, who planned to entertain the King on her husband's estate near Dublin, Castlereagh was not allowed to bring his wife with him. Nor did the King, with whom he was not on particularly good terms at this time, invite his Foreign Minister to accompany him on the first part of the journey from Portsmouth to Holyhead, which was made in his 'yatch' (as he spelled it) the *Royal George*, a sailing vessel of some 340 tons which does not seem to have been very seaworthy.

Castlereagh and Sidmouth travelled to Holyhead by post-chaise and for once they were agreeably impressed by their reception on the road. 'To my surprise it began at Coventry, which was the first great town we reached,' Castlereagh wrote to his wife at Cray. 'The mob were assembled round the inn and, with two exceptions who called out "Queen", cheered us on arrival and departure. At Birmingham the collection of people was much larger and of the most respectable description, and the reception most cordial and unanimous. At Wolverhampton and Shifnal the same, but what most proved the change of public sentiment was my reception at Shrewsbury (Burdett's town), where a great concourse assembled round the inn whilst we were at dinner and cheered us in the warmest manner; indeed the sentiment seemed general throughout the streets of the towns by whence we passed. It is impossible to have a more decisive proof that our friend John [Bull] has recovered his senses.'

His next stop after Shrewsbury was Llangollen, where he paused to pay his respects to the two 'most celebrated virgins in Europe', or the 'ladies of Llangollen' as Miss Sarah Ponsonby and Lady Eleanor Butler were known. Castlereagh had kept in touch with them ever since the day, thirty-five years before, when they had been introduced by his father on his way to take up his residence as an undergraduate at Cambridge. 'This morning we breakfasted with our old friends at the Cottage, who were full of enquiries after you,' he wrote to Emily on 8th August 1821. 'They are in surprising preservation.' He promised to send them 'a print' of himself 'to hang up' at Plas Newydd. 'Pray order one to be smartly framed and sent well packed by the Coach to their address.'

The Queen's life was rapidly ebbing away when Castlereagh left London. 'What a singular close,' he wrote to his brother, 'if Providence should effect that divorce, in attempting which every human effort failed.' The Foreign Secretary's arrival in Holyhead coincided with the appearance of an express messenger from London bearing the expected news of Her Majesty's death. No doubt it was partly on this account that the King now behaved in a more friendly fashion to the Minister, in fact 'embargoed me', as Castlereagh put it, 'and ordered me to proceed with him to Dublin' in the *Royal George*. In the meantime Sidmouth had taken passage in the regular steam packet. 'I am very comfortably lodged on board of this yacht,' Castlereagh wrote next day, 'and slept sound last night notwithstanding the noise and the hardness of my bed.' As for the late Queen, her departure from her troubled life naturally involved some changes in the royal programme in Ireland, since in the circumstances His Majesty could not very well appear in public until after his late wife's funeral had taken place. Otherwise, remarked Castlereagh, 'the King has been very reasonable in lending himself to every proper arrangement on this occasion and bears his *good fortune* with great propriety'. The unfortunate Caroline had been a sore trial to the Minister during her lifetime, so that it was not altogether surprising that he should have regarded her death as 'the greatest of all possible deliverances for His Majesty and the country'.

Contrary winds held up the royal party for three days. 'Don't think us both mad if we should go over in a steamboat,' wrote Castlereagh to Emily. And again, two days later, 'We are still wind-bound, my dearest Em, but I regret it the less, as the King is decorously quiet here. . . . H.M. dined with us yesterday and was in good health and spirits, longing however to get over.' Eventually the *Royal George* set sail early in the morning of Sunday 12th August, and about three o'clock the same afternoon was sighted some distance off the harbour of Dunleary, which the local authorities had already decided to rename Kingstown in honour of the occasion. On landing at the pier an hour and a half later, His Majesty was given a rousing welcome by the crowds which had been lining the shore from early morning. Among the spectators, the King, who was dressed in a blue frock-coat, blue pantaloons, Hessian boots, a black cravat, white silk gloves and a forage-cap with gold lace, recognised several old friends. Castlereagh, who was in immediate attendance, also recognised them. Catching sight of the Earl of Kingston, His Majesty exclaimed: 'Kingston, Kingston, you black-whiskered, good-natured fellow, I am happy to see you in this friendly country.' Another friend, Mr. Denis Bowes-Daly, was in the act of shaking hands with His Majesty when he had the misfortune to be deprived of his pocket-book and a watch valued at sixty guineas. In the process of disembarking His Majesty, several of the loyal gentry who attempted to get on to the royal yacht fell into the water in an intoxication of loyalty and alcohol.

The King drove with Castlereagh and the rest of his entourage to the Viceroy's Lodge in Phoenix Park, there to spend, in Castlereagh's words, 'the proper number of days before he makes his public appearance'. When he alighted in the Park, the royal carriage was immediately surrounded by another crowd. 'This is one of the happiest moments in my life,' said His Majesty in a graceful impromptu speech. 'I feel pleased, being the first of my family that set foot on Irish ground. . . . I rejoice at being among my faithful Irish friends. I always considered them such, and this day proves to me I am beloved by them . . . I assure you, my dear friends, I have an Irish heart, and will this night give proof of my affection towards you, as I am sure you will towards me, by drinking your health in a bumper of whiskey punch.'

The next few days the King spent quietly with Lord Talbot, the Lord Lieutenant, and his suite—that is, until the Queen's remains had left England for her native Brunswick and his advisers judged it proper for him to venture forth in public. He made his State entry into Dublin on 17th August, and it was perhaps the greatest personal triumph of his life. His Majesty, accompanied by the two Ministers, was seated in an open barouche drawn by eight horses, while in his hat was displayed an enormous shamrock to which he repeatedly pointed. In the midst of the shouting he declared to his Private Secretary, Sir Benjamin Bloomfield, who was an Irishman, that he might be proud of his country: 'they are a noble people'. As he looked out on the acclaiming multitudes from the windows of Dublin Castle, he was observed to shed tears. When Lord Sidmouth expressed wonder at the patent loyalty of a people who had recently been in rebellion, the King replied, 'Not at all! Their former character must have been caused by misrule'. There followed illuminations, reviews, a visit to the theatre, a ball at the Mansion House and even a day's racing at the Curragh, as well as excursions to Powerscourt and Slane Castle, seat of the Conynghams. He discussed the Act of Union quite frankly with some of the Irish gentry, whom he met at one of these functions. 'You all committed a great mistake,' he told them. 'You should have made terms as the Scotch did; and you could have got any terms.' 'And the Scotch further stipulated for the establishment of their national religion,' remarked a former Member of the old Irish Parliament. 'You are right,' said the King. 'They secured that point also.'

At the end of a week Castlereagh wrote to his wife:

Never did Providence preside over any barren transaction more auspiciously than over this visit to Ireland. It has been without alloy—everything perfect. I have not seen a drunken man in the streets. I have not heard an unkind word from a single individual, and yet I have mixed unsparingly with the people and the effect is not less strong in the remote parts of Ireland where every village has been illuminated for the King's arrival.

A gentleman met a poor Paddy from this part of Ireland in the streets of Dublin and asked him what had brought him to town. 'Sure, your Honour, I came to see the King.' 'But what made you come above a hundred miles on such an errand?' 'Why, to be sure it was a good walk, but I thought nothing of it, when I considered how much further His Majesty, long life to him, had come to see me!'

He also wrote to Mrs. Arbuthnot that His Majesty's public entry into Dublin beat the Coronation not in splendour of dresses but in the crowds and enthusiasm of the people' The King. raves of Ireland,' he told her, adding that George said he would like to take up his abode there and send Lord Talbot to London as his Lord Lieutenant.

Castlereagh was included in the house-party at Slane Castle—as a Minister in attendance on His Majesty he could not very well have been omitted, although his hostess no doubt invited him with considerable reluctance—but he stayed no longer than one night. 'The King's passion for the place is equal to that for the proprietress,' he told his wife afterwards; 'greater it cannot be.' The party included William Plunket, a relative of Lord Conyngham's, who had been conspicuous for his bitter and fiery oratory in the Union Debates and in particular for his attacks on Castlereagh in the former Irish House of Commons twenty years before. He had once described Castlereagh, who was then Chief Secretary to the Lord Lieutenant, as 'a green and sapless twig' on the floor of the House, with the childless Emily looking on from the gallery. But these old personal animosities seem to have been forgotten on this occasion. Anyhow Plunket had taken a job from the British Government and was then Lord Chancellor of Ireland. Nevertheless, in Castlereagh's words, 'the evening was most royally dull' and he was glad to escape next day to Mount Stewart.

What made this visit to Ireland so memorable—it was to be his last—was his reception in his native city, so different from the old days. Then, in addition to the diatribes of Plunket and other leading anti-Unionists, the mob had burned him in effigy outside his house in Merrion Square and then proceeded to break all the windows. Now he came in for a remarkable share of the general acclamation. He was cheered tumultuously, and the people even attempted to chair him through the streets. 'I am grown as popular in 1821 as unpopular formerly, and with as little merit,' was his characteristic remark; 'and of the two, unpopularity is the more convenient and gentlemanlike.' The Whig Opposition newspapers in England were particularly angry at this enthusiastic reception, and they discovered an ingenious reason to explain this. Castlereagh had recently succeeded to his father's Irish marquisate and he was naturally addressed by this title throughout the visit. This gave the papers their clue. In Mrs. Arbuthnot's words, 'They pretend to fancy the people don't know Lord Londonderry *was* Lord Castlereagh.'

CHAPTER FIVE

The Mystery Explained

I

'DON'T BE HARD ON CASTLEREAGH, for he too loves Ireland.' Thus the Irish patriot Henry Grattan advised his son on entering the House of Commons. He repeated this advice on his death-bed. 'The Union is past,' he said, 'the business between me and him is over, and it is for the interest of Ireland that Lord Castlereagh should be Minister.' Yet, in spite of this injunction, the legend of 'Bloody Castlereagh' has died hard in the country of his birth. Many tears have come to patriot eyes and many lumps have formed in patriot throats at the thought of the national liberties once enshrined in the old Parliament House in Dublin. But the architectural beauties of this building were, and still are, probably its greatest feature. As an assembly it was thoroughly corrupt and largely unrepresentative of Ireland; no one professing the Roman Catholic faith—the faith of the majority in the country—was ever permitted to sit in it. Barely ten years after the Act, which united the two countries politically, had reached the statute-book, Castlereagh had written to Alexander Knox, his former private secretary in Ireland: 'The demons of the present day are at work to make those who carried the Union odious, as first having cruelly oppressed and then sold their country. The world's forgetfulness of the events which are a few years gone by enable them to mislead numbers. . . . I feel confident that the intentions of Government for the public good at that time will bear the strictest scrutiny. . . . I believe their measures when fairly explained, will stand equally the test of criticism; and that they may be shown to have combined humanity with vigour of administration, when they had to watch over the preservation of the State, while in the conduct of the Union they pursued honestly the interests of Ireland, yielding not more to private interests than was requisite to disarm so mighty a change of any convulsive character.'

The most serious charge brought against Castlereagh's memory and reputation has been that he was personally implicated in the cruelties and excesses committed against the rebels and suspected rebels during the rising of 1798. When talk of blackmail was going the rounds a quarter of a century later, some people thought that it might have concerned some horrible activity on the part of the former Chief Secretary for Ireland at that period. Did not the Nationalist poet Tom Moore commemorate his part in 'the bloody transactions of '98'?

> And that the Irish—grateful nation!—
> Remember when by *thee* reigned over,
> And bless thee for their flagellation
> As Heloisa did her lover.

And for saying as much, with rather more particularity, an Irish journalist had been convicted of criminally libelling Castlereagh and sent to prison. In 1810, Peter Finnerty, a former war correspondent for the *Morning Chronicle*, accused Castlereagh of 'having sanctioned torture' and of 'having been guilty of tyranny, cruelty and oppression in the administration of the Government of Ireland'. In an affidavit sworn by one of Finnerty's friends the deponent stated that 'in the year 1798 various kinds of torture such as whippings, picketings, half-hangings, etc., etc., were practised in Dublin close to the Castle Gate' and, moreover, that

'Lord Castlereagh could have heard the cries of the sufferers in his office'.

Peter Finnerty was an eccentric Irishman, quick-witted, hot-tempered and rash. He had been in trouble fourteen years previously for publishing a seditious libel at the beginning of Castlereagh's Ministerial career in Ireland. On that occasion, besides a prison term, he had been sentenced to stand in the pillory outside the principal criminal courts in Dublin. 'My friends, you see how cheerfully I can suffer,' this whole-hearted republican exclaimed to the immense concourse of sympathising spectators. 'I can suffer anything provided it promotes the liberty of my country.' Besides the pillory and a fine of £20, he suffered five years in prison on that occasion. For libelling Castlereagh in 1810 he spent a further eighteen months in Lincoln Gaol, where his alleged ill-treatment by his gaolers led to a lively discussion in the House of Commons. Castlereagh bore him no ill will—he was a back-bencher then—and even pleaded for the mitigation of his punishment. But at the same time he flatly denied Finnerty's libellous charges, admitting his readiness if necessary 'to prove to the satisfaction of the House and the country that the general conduct of the Irish administration (he spoke not of individual instances of cruelty which nothing could justify) was at that time fully justifiable'.

For some years the matter had rested. Then Brougham unexpectedly chose to raise it on the last day of the parliamentary session in 1817. Although Castlereagh was taken somewhat by surprise, Brougham had informed some of his Opposition friends of his intention in advance, since one of them read out several of Finnerty's affidavits and then went on to assert that if Castlereagh and his colleagues in the Irish Government had not flogged their miserable victims with their own hands, 'they were at least guilty of having not only not punished those who had perpetrated these enormities, but of having singled them out as fit objects for reward'.

The reference here was to a former High Sheriff of County Tipperary, by name Thomas Judkin-Fitzgerald, who had been indemnified by the Irish House of Commons for having exceeded his authority on numerous occasions during the rebellion of 1798. His system was to flog every suspected rebel 'till he told the truth', inasmuch that on his own admission in court, when he was successfully sued for assault, 'men who refused to give any information on his first taking them up did after some flogging make ample discoveries'. In fact this remarkable Irish officer of the law went so far as to state publicly that he considered himself justified in applying every method to obtain confessions from suspected rebels, and that 'in order to discover the truth, if every other method failed, he had a right to cut off their heads'.

It is true that Judkin-Fitzgerald subsequently received a pension from the Irish Government and was created a baronet, but these awards took place after Castlereagh's resignation as Chief Secretary for Ireland and he was not instrumental in recommending him. Nor did he take any part in promoting the indemnification proceedings; on the contrary he stated at the time that he 'could not conceive that any man should be indemnified who appears to a jury to have acted maliciously, and in which opinion the Bench concurs'. In reply to the debate on Brougham's motion in 1817, Castlereagh very properly asked why he had not long since been brought to trial for the cruelties alleged to have been committed by himself and his colleagues in Ireland, if they were believed to be true. He could not deny, of course, that summary modes of corporal punishment had been employed by the military forces in Ireland in the suppression of the rebellion, but he declared that he had never been present at any of these punishments. In fact, he had never in the course of his life seen any man flogged, he added, except a soldier in his own militia regiment.

'With respect to Ireland, I know I never shall be forgiven,' he said. 'I have with many others incurred the inexpiable guilt of preserving that main branch of the British Empire from that separation which the traitors of Ireland, in conjunction with a foreign power, had meditated. . . . Those who were foiled in their attempt have consoled themselves by endeavouring, as far as they could, to throw calumny on my name and character. For what reason? Because I exerted myself to defend the people of Ireland from the conspiracy which surrounded them. My conduct has been the constant theme of invective. But I think those who are acquainted with me will do me the justice to believe that I never had a cruel or unkind heart.'

A long period was to elapse before Brougham could bring himself to admit that his judgment in the matter was at fault. But in 1839 he admitted his error. In his *Historical Sketches of the Reign of George the Third*, which appeared in that year, he put it on record that 'Lord Castlereagh uniformly and strenuously set his face against the atrocities committed in Ireland' and that 'to him, more than perhaps anyone else, was to be attributed the termination of the system stained with blood'.

2

One of the contributory factors to Castlereagh's suicide, according to popular gossip at the time, was an element of mental instability in his family. 'Lord Londonderry's mother was a Seymour-Conway,' noted Henry Hobhouse, the Permanent Under-Secretary at the Home Office, in his diary on the day of the funeral, 'in which family there is undoubtedly an hereditary taint'. According to the Comtesse de Boigne, daughter of the French Ambassador in London at the time, 'his death can only be attributed to a fit of madness which was hereditary in his family'.

On his father's side Castlereagh came of solid Ulster-Scots stock, Presbyterians by religion. There was a story current during his lifetime that his paternal grandfather, Alexander Stewart of Ballylawn, Co. Donegal, who laid the financial foundation of the family fortunes by marrying a rich heiress from Londonderry, called Mary Cowan, was a pedlar who had come over from Scotland with a pack on his back in the early years of the previous century and whose real name was MacGregor. While the story about the immigrant pedlar can easily be disproved from authentic family records, as well as by the Stewart pedigree which was accepted and registered by the Irish College of Heralds in Dublin, there are grounds for believing that Castlereagh was descended in the direct male line from a member of the Clan Mac-Gregor, who was living in Dumbartonshire at the beginning of the seventeenth century and changed his name to Stewart consequent upon the proscription of the clan and the prohibition of the use of the name by King James I in or about the year 1603. (It was the MacGregors who also supplied the legendary Rob Roy, the hero of Sir Walter Scott's novel of the same name.) The original Stewart or MacGregor, known as Alexander Macaulay, who obtained the Donegal estate during the Plantation of Ulster at this time, had a son John, who was confirmed in the grant of the property. It was his great-great-grandson, Alexander, the supposed pedlar, who married the heiress Mary Cowan. She was the sister of Sir Robert Cowan, who was Governor of Bombay and amassed the fortune which she inherited, in the service of the East India Company. Alexander Stewart and his wife were the parents of Robert, the first Lord Londonderry and father of Castlereagh. It was this same Alexander Stewart who bought the Mount Stewart estate in County Down and began to build the demesne house, which his son completed.

Robert Stewart, who was born a commoner in 1739 and

died Marquess of Londonderry in 1821, married Lady Sarah Seymour-Conway, daughter of the Earl of Hertford, Lord Lieutenant of Ireland at the time and a considerable landowner in Ulster, where his rents brought him in £15,000 a year. The marriage took place in the Chapel Royal in Dublin Castle. The bride, who had not yet reached her nineteenth birthday, was, we are told on contemporary authority, 'admired for her fine person and accomplishments and beloved for the unaffected goodness of her mind and manners'. She seems to have been a young woman of exceptional physical beauty, and it was no doubt from her that Castlereagh, who was her second and only surviving child, inherited his own handsome looks. She appears to have been in every respect a perfectly normal person. That there were, however, evidences of eccentricity, not to say abnormality, in the Seymour-Conway family, is beyond dispute. They certainly appeared in her nephew, later Lord Hertford, who sat in the House of Commons as Earl of Yarmouth with his cousin Castlereagh, and acted as his cousin's second when Castlereagh fought his celebrated pistol duel with Canning on Putney Heath. Yarmouth, on whom Thackeray modelled his original of his character 'The Marquess of Steyne' in *Vanity Fair*, lived with a retinue of prostitutes and was described in his later years by Charles Greville as 'broken with various infirmities and almost unintelligible from paralysis of the tongue'. According to this diarist, 'there has been, so far as I know, no such example of undisguised debauchery exhibited to the world'.

After the wedding, Mr. Robert and Lady Sarah Stewart settled in Dublin in a house in Henry Street, afterwards pulled down to make room for the present General Post Office. It was in this house that Castlereagh was born on the 18th June 1769, the day on which Napoleon was finally defeated at Waterloo forty-six years later by Castlereagh's fellow Irishman, Arthur Wellesley, Duke of Wellington, whose career Castlereagh as War Minister had, as we have seen, so conspicuously furthered. Castlereagh was the second son, but his elder brother died in infancy in the same month of his birth, so that he had immediately become his father's heir. The newly-born was called Robert, after his father, and was baptised a Presbyterian in the neighbouring church of the 'Protestant Dissenting Congregation' in Strand Street. While his father always remained a Presbyterian, Castlereagh was to embrace the Established Church in his youth: otherwise he could not have gained admission as an undergraduate to St. John's College, Cambridge.

Castlereagh never knew his beautiful mother in the flesh, as she died in giving birth to a stillborn child a few days after his second birthday. But he knew her likeness, which she bequeathed to him in the form of a miniature, with some strands of her hair. Castlereagh incorporated these in a brooch, inscribed with the one word 'Irreparable', which he always wore and only laid aside at the time of his last illness.

Six years after Sarah's death the elder Robert Stewart married for the second time, Lady Frances Pratt, daughter of the ex-Lord Chancellor Lord Camden. Thus he succeeded in allying himself with two of the most powerful Whig families in England and established connections which were to be instrumental in advancing the fortunes of both himself and his children, of whom ten were by his second wife. In 1789, through Lord Hertford's influence, he was raised to the peerage as Lord Londonderry, with the rank of Baron in the peerage of Ireland, while during the next seven years, through the offices of his brother-in-law, Lord Camden, who now occupied the Viceregal Lodge in Dublin, he was successively created Viscount Castlereagh and Earl of Londonderry. It was the latter advancement, bestowed in

1796, that carried the courtesy title of Viscount Castlereagh for his eldest son. In 1801 he became one of the twenty-eight Irish representative peers, elected for life, with the right to sit in the House of Lords at Westminster. His final step in the peerage, to Marquess, took place in 1816, in recognition of his son's diplomatic achievements at Paris and Vienna. Though not a record in the ascent of the ladder of honours, the progress from commoner to Marquess in a little over twenty-five years was remarkable even for those times.

The first Robert Stewart admitted at the time that he had no desire to be further ennobled. He was content to lead a quiet existence on his estate in County Down and contemplate his son's Ministerial progress. On his daughter-in-law's return to England from Paris, where she had gone with Castlereagh for the negotiations of the first treaty of peace, the old man could scarcely believe his ears at the news he heard. 'I offer you my most sincere and hearty congratulations on your early and safe return to London,' he wrote to her, 'after the very singular and interesting excursion in which you have been engaged on the Continent, the wonderful change and revolution which you are witness to in France. It must have afforded a scene equally novel and curious, and the volatile deportment, so peculiarly characteristic of the Nation, must have added not a little to the singularity of the awful crisis which had brought such mighty sovereigns into the same metropolis to arrange and settle the peace of Europe. But what above all must have been gratifying to you was to see that your dear husband was lately to succeed in fulfilling the difficult and momentous duties entrusted to him, which have been so unquestionably verified on his return both by the gracious reception and honours conferred upon him by the Prince Regent, as well as the unbounded national applause and general expressions of gratitude poured out by his countrymen. . . . I can well imagine how much you share and partake in my paternal delirium, which sometimes so works on my imagination I can scarcely refrain from saying—Is all this really true?'

3

The novelist Sir Walter Scott once remarked to the Irish poet Tom Moore that 'the only two men who had ever told him that they had actually seen a ghost afterwards put an end to themselves—one was Lord Castlereagh'. The occasion on which Scott heard Castlereagh relate the story of the ghost was during a supper-party given by Lady Castlereagh in Paris in 1815, when the Foreign Minister did so with a gravity which astonished his listeners. The apparition, which Castlereagh called 'The Radiant Boy' and which he was apparently in the habit of describing in conversation, had revealed itself to him more than twenty years previously while he was soldiering with his militia regiment in the west of Ireland.

The incident of 'The Radiant Boy' occurred about the year 1793 in the small town of Ballyshannon in County Donegal, where the Londonderry Militia, which Lieutenant-Colonel Robert Stewart, as he then was, commanded, was quartered for the winter in anticipation of a possible French invasion. Returning late one evening with his men to their barracks after a long field-day, he said he felt tired and in low spirits. A fire of wood and peat blazed in the large open fire-place in the room where he slept, and after contemplating it in solitude for some time after supper he went to bed. He awoke some time during the night, and for a while lay watching from his pillow the gradual darkening of the embers on the hearth. Suddenly the embers began to burn up brightly, and then—according to Castlereagh—the figure of a naked male child stepped out into the room. The apparition advanced slowly towards the bed, increasing in

size at every step, until on coming within a few paces of him
—so runs Sir Walter Scott's account—'it had assumed the
appearance of a ghastly giant with a bleeding wound on the
brow and eyes glaring with rage and despair'. The young
militia officer immediately jumped out of bed and, as Scott
put it, 'confronted the figure in an attitude of defiance'. It
thereupon retreated, gradually growing smaller and assum-
ing its original childlike form. It then disappeared into the
fire, and Castlereagh went back to bed.

Next day he recounted the experience to his brother
officers. They were inclined to dismiss it as a bad dream.
Nevertheless the legend of 'The Radiant Boy' persisted for
long afterwards in the neighbourhood, and visitors to the old
house by the bridge at Ballyshannon used to be shown the
room where the vision was supposed to have appeared. The
poet William Allingham, who was born in Ballyshannon in
1824 and brought up in the neighbourhood, heard the tale
in his childhood and later recorded it in verse. His account
concludes with these lines:

> This happened when our island still
> Had nests of goblins left, to fill
> Each mouldy nook and corner close,
> Like spiders in an ancient house.
> And this one read within the face
> Intruding on its dwelling place,
> Lines of woe, despair and blood,
> By spirits only understood;
> As mortals now can read the same
> In the letters of his name,
> Who in that haunted chamber lay
> When we call him—Castlereagh.

The only occasion on which Castlereagh is known to have
become a prey to the imaginary fears which beset him so

pathetically during the last days of his life, occurred a few years after the episode of 'The Radiant Boy', in the spring of 1801, when he became seriously ill in London with a raging fever and the doctor who attended him at one moment despaired of his life. According to Henry Hobhouse, writing at the time of his death in 1822, 'the anxiety which Lord Londonderry underwent in negotiating the Union with Ireland, followed by the change of Ministry before many of the pecuniary arrangements which he had made in the course of that negotiation were discharged, produced such an effect upon him that he was affected with a brain fever in 1801, from which he did not recover until Mr. Addington agreed to take on himself the fulfilment of those engagements'.

For the first time, on New Year's Day 1801 the new Union Jack, which bore the Cross of Saint Patrick in addition to those of Saint George and Saint Andrew, had flown from the walls of Dublin Castle. It was generally thought throughout Ireland that a legislative union with Great Britain would be immediately followed by a measure relieving His Majesty's Roman Catholic subjects of their disabilities. Castlereagh had promised as much on the authority of the Prime Minister, Mr. Pitt, and he had already sketched out the draft of such a measure when he took his seat in the United Parliament at Westminster. But he and the other advocates of Catholic emancipation had reckoned without the Sovereign, who obstinately clung to the view that if he gave his royal assent to such a measure, it would violate his Coronation oath. At a levée which he held towards the end of January 1801, George III had picked out the thirty-one-year-old Chief Secretary for Ireland in the throng of courtiers and declared that he considered the proposal to emancipate the Catholics as 'the most Jacobinical thing he had ever heard of'. 'What is this that this young Lord has brought over and which they are going to throw at my head?' he had asked a friend. 'I shall reckon any man my personal enemy who proposes any such measure.'

There was no alternative for Pitt but to resign his office of Prime Minister. Castlereagh and Cornwallis, the Lord Lieutenant of Ireland, did likewise and soon the Dublin mob was chanting:

> A high gallows and a windy day
> For Billy Pitt and Castlereagh.

The new Prime Minister was the future Viscount Sidmouth, then Mr. Henry Addington, M.P., Speaker of the House of Commons. In becoming the tenant of No. 10 Downing Street, Addington thus achieved the highest political power without ever having held previous Ministerial office of any kind, not even a Junior Lordship of the Treasury. His reign as head of the Government was destined to be short. He left Downing Street two years later never to return as Prime Minister, although he was subsequently a member of several Tory administrations and sat with Castlereagh in Lord Liverpool's Cabinet.

As a boy, Castlereagh had for a time been regarded as 'delicate'. Some years after his death, his old tutor, the Rev. James Cleland, recalled to his widow that he had 'received him at the age of ten, a sickly enfeebled child and wasted in the left arm by an issue long previously applied'. But he had grown stronger with the years, and it was not until he was thirty-one years old that he had what appears to have been his first serious illness, when a high temperature was combined with acute anxiety following on the political changes described above. While the Act of Union had given fair compensation to those who lost their offices or their property as a result of the extinction of the separate Irish Parliament, there were some minor vested interests which had not been expressly provided for in the statute, and it was in respect of these that Addington put Castlereagh's mind at rest by undertaking to honour the promises he had made. These payments, it may be added, had not been in any sense bribes, but simply compensation to dispossessed office-holders.

Castlereagh's illness at this time had worried his family and friends a good deal. 'I have been, and indeed am still, very uneasy about Lord Castlereagh, who has had a return of his fever,' wrote Lord Cornwallis at the beginning of May. 'They tell me there is no danger, but I have never heard of a fever of so long continuance without danger.' But he eventually recovered and went north to Harrogate to convalesce for two months. 'I have been very idle since I came,' he wrote at the end of July, 'have forgot politics and am grown very fat.' Restored to health, he was unable to forget politics for long. In the following year, he joined Addington's Government as President of the Board of Control, in charge of Indian affairs; with the exception of three years following his duel with Canning when he was out of office, he was to sit on the Treasury Bench for the remainder of his life, being Leader of the House of Commons as well as Foreign Secretary for the last ten years.

As has been seen, it was not until the final month or two of his life that marked eccentricities in his behaviour began to be noted by observers. But there was one curious incident, which took place towards the end of the war with France and was remembered afterwards. Castlereagh invited Wellington's brother-in-law, Sir Edward Pakenham, a distinguished soldier who had been Adjutant-General in the Peninsular War and who was on his way to North America, to breakfast with him one morning in St. James's Square. Pakenham had promised to introduce his doctor, whose name was Howell, to the Foreign Minister, and the doctor was accordingly included in the invitation. When the meal was over, Castlereagh asked Dr. Howell exactly where the jugular vein was situated. The doctor explained it to his host's satisfaction, stating that it would be a dangerous experiment for any man to take the slightest liberty with that artery, 'for death would inevitably follow if it were pierced'. 'Indeed?' rejoined Castlereagh carelessly. 'You must think me very ignorant but I am rather curious in such matters.'

As the doctor concluded his explanation Pakenham noticed a peculiar look about the Foreign Minister. Later, when they were walking back together to their hotel, he mentioned it to his companion. 'I am afraid, Doctor, you were too explicit about the jugular artery,' Pakenham remarked, 'for I observed Castlereagh to be in a strange mood when you finished your anatomical lecture.'

About a year later, a few weeks after Waterloo, Castlereagh happened to meet Thomas Creevey, the Whig diarist and M.P., at a ball given by the Duke of Wellington in Paris. They had just heard that their House of Commons colleague, Samuel Whitbread, the brewer, had killed himself in London by cutting his throat. As Creevey was to recall afterwards, Castlereagh came up to him and asked him if he 'had not been greatly surprised at Whitbread's death and the manner of it'. Then, noted Mr. Creevey, 'we had a good deal of conversation on the subject'.

Be that as it may, it was remarked at the time of Castlereagh's death that the act of suicide was accomplished with anatomical precision.

4

At the end of 1821, Castlereagh appeared as complete master of himself and showed no sign of the burden which he had borne both as Foreign Minister and Leader of the House of Commons for nearly ten years. 'Londonderry goes on as usual,' wrote his colleague John Wilson Croker, M.P., Parliamentary Secretary to the Admiralty, on 21st December, 'and like Mont Blanc continues to gather all the sunshine upon his icy head. He is *better* than ever; that is, colder, steadier, more *procurante*, and withal more amiable and respected. It is a splendid summit of bright and polished frost which, like the travellers in Switzerland, we all admire; but which no one can hope, and few would wish, to reach.'

During the next five months the machine began to run down, although it was not until towards the end of May 1822 that anything amiss with the Minister began to be noticed. Early in the New Year he met Mrs. Arbuthnot at several country-house parties, and appeared in good spirits. At a shoot at Ashridge, Lord Bridgewater's estate in Hertfordshire, Castlereagh invariably had the largest bag and on one day accounted for 107 birds. Parliament met as usual, early in February, with some of the Tory country gentlemen showing signs of discontent, but the Leader of the House succeeded in mollifying them with a promise of a committee to regulate the import of foreign corn. However, the country gentlemen continued in a rebellious frame of mind and early in the session combined with the Opposition to defeat the Government on an Admiralty matter. Mrs. Arbuthnot urged Castlereagh to have a meeting with the country members to tell them plainly that if they would not support the Government on details of policy, they might have to face a change of Ministers. 'Lord Londonderry is so good-natured that I dare say he will not do this,' noted Mrs. Arbuthnot in her journal; 'he says they only give these votes occasionally to make a figure in the columns of the Opposition papers and please their constituents and they trust to good luck that their votes will only lessen [and] not overturn our majority.' It was on this occasion when discussing the defection of the country members that the Minister for the first time confided in Mrs. Arbuthnot that he 'was tired of office and wished he could slip his neck out of the yoke'. She afterwards recalled that at this period 'he appeared always languid and worn and out of spirits'.

On 29th April 1822 Castlereagh introduced in the House of Commons a number of resolutions designed to relieve the prevailing agricultural distress in the country. 'As usual in making a statement,' Mrs. Arbuthnot remarked at the time, 'Lord Londonderry was so confused and involved in his language that the House did not the least understand it, with the exception of Brougham who comprehended it perfectly and showed the greatest acuteness in arguing upon it. . . . He never, I think, displayed more acuteness and financial quickness than in thus seizing the meaning of a plan so wretchedly expressed by Lord Londonderry.'

The first serious signs of breakdown came, as we have seen, during the dispute about the King's dinner to the Princess of Denmark, when Princess Lieven detected a startling change in the Minister's appearance. It was about the same time that Castlereagh, happening to be riding in Hyde Park, encountered a back-bench M.P., Lord Tavistock. Although he had no more than a nodding acquaintance with this member, nevertheless he turned his horse about and proceeded to unburden himself on public affairs. According to Mr. Creevey, 'he described the *torment* of carrying on the Government under the general circumstances of the country as beyond endurance, and said if he could once get out of it, no power on earth should get him into it again'.

"You don't often come amongst us," Castlereagh remarked to his surprised fellow member, as he rode away. "I don't wonder at it."

Although Castlereagh was an indifferent speaker and frequently amused the House by the tortuous language he employed, he had a remarkable memory; he usually spoke without notes, and he was often able to recall, with an accuracy which astonished his audience, particulars of proceedings which had taken place many years previously. About six weeks before the final tragedy, his memory suddenly failed. The incident which attracted attention to this occurred in the House early in July.

An account had appeared in all the newspapers of the capture under an obsolete Spanish law of an English trading-ship bound for Buenos Aires by a Spanish vessel. The British ship had been taken to Puerto Rico and there condemned as prize. A private member, Sir James Mackintosh, asked the Foreign Secretary what steps he was taking to prevent the recurrence of a similar injury to the mercantile marine in the future.

It was impossible that Castlereagh could not have heard of the capture, which had been reported to the Foreign Office before news of it got into the press. Indeed, a document relating to it was actually lying on the table in front of him at the time. Yet, to the astonishment of the House, he rose from his place on the Treasury Bench and declared he had never heard of the matter. If it had occurred, he went on, he would be obliged to any honourable member who could make him acquainted with the particulars of it.

At this statement Dr. Stephen Lushington, M.P., an authority on international law, got up and said that he had seen the decree of condemnation and would be glad to furnish Castlereagh with a copy of it. The Foreign Secretary thereupon expressed his thanks, adding that he would be glad to peruse it, as the document in question had never been in his possession.

'This fact,' noted his brother Stewart, in recalling the incident afterwards, 'may be fairly taken as a distressing proof of that declension of memory, or listlessness of mind, which but too truly demonstrates a loss of intellect.'

Stewart, who had been on leave from his post in Vienna that summer, left London to return to Austria on 18th July.

On that day or the previous day he called at Castlereagh's house in St. James's Square to say good-bye to his brother. When he heard the news of the tragedy, he was still on the road, and in writing to his sister-in-law he dwelt on the worries caused by the activities of Lady Conyngham at Court, which, as we have seen, he had come up against at close quarters and which he was inclined to think provided the last straw.

'That he was of late under a pressure of spirits unusual to him, I have long been aware,' he wrote to Emily Lady Londonderry on 25th August, as soon as he reached Vienna. 'But this was well accounted for, not only from the slavery of his public duty, but more particularly from those miserable intrigues, and that royal conduct which wounded him in the tenderest and most acute quarter . . . In late times, however, he sorely felt the undue influence that has so shamefully preponderated. I consider much of the intrigues that were carried on this year by the women surrounding the King gave additional friction to all his other torments, so that he had not a moment of tranquil repose, and we all know that human nature has only a certain power and if exhausted will fail. I have mentioned the above circumstances because it has been the first year in which he ever admitted to me that the toils of office had become too burdensome to him and that he must positively soon look to a new arrangement and more repose. Still, when we last parted, I flattered myself (in your drawing-room that day) he never looked better, and his letters to me up to the 2nd August are written in the fullest, clearest manner and with his usual comprehensive detail.'

It is noteworthy that his brother-in-law Sir Henry Hardinge M.P. attributed the cause of the breakdown to 'dormant gout', from which Castlereagh had long been suffering, adding that 'it unfortunately rose to his head and affected the intellect until removed or dispersed'. On this point Castlereagh had himself more than once during the parliamentary session apparently wished the gout would show itself by pain in his limbs, and he complained of oppression and was convinced his general health would improve 'if the gout would shew itself'.

'I state these things', wrote Hardinge to Stewart on the day of the funeral, 'because, although I believe that this state of illness was generated by his excessive attention to business and want of exercise, I do not believe that his intellect had received any injury further than that temporary derangement incidental to a bad state of bodily health, and in this view the Duke of Wellington, Fred Robinson, Planta, and all those with whom I have spoken concur. Others trace it as having made a more progressive advance; but this, except by Lady Londonderry herself, does not appear to be borne out by facts. His last speeches in the House were admirable. He dined with us the 25th and 26th July and was cheerful. His colleagues, his secretaries, observed nothing previous to the beginning of this month, and as far as assumption of opinion can go, I should agree with the Duke that his great mind had not given way, but that he was latterly suffering under a specific positive disorder of a bodily nature, as temporary as any other fever or attack of gout. The Duke said his influence with the King up to the last interview of Friday (8th August] continued, and that he thought his views for the last twelve months were sounder and clearer than he had ever known them.'

The last time he addressed the House of Commons was on 30th July, when he spoke at some length, and with evident clarity, on the subject of Spanish piracy in the West Indies. On the previous day he wrote several private letters from his room in the Foreign Office, including one to his brother Charles Stewart in Vienna, and the other to the Austrian Chancellor, Prince Metternich. Though not illegible, the handwriting was rather more cursive than usual and certainly indicated traces of strain. However, the language in which they were expressed was quite clear.

'The King has fixed his departure for Scotland on the 9th of next month,' he wrote in his letter to Metternich, 'and I have received His Majesty's commands (should no unforeseen event arise) to set out about the 15th for Vienna. I calculate upon arriving about the 7th of September, passing by Paris where I shall stop for three or four days. As Lady Londonderry will accompany me (being particularly desirous of paying her respects to her many kind friends in that capital), my journey will not be performed with the celerity of a courier, but I shall take care to regulate my march so as to have some days at my disposal for preliminary conversation, before the arrival of the Sovereigns.'

The unforeseen event which prevented the Foreign Secretary's journey from taking place as planned occurred a fortnight after he wrote this letter.

5

Following the tragedy, criticism of neglect during the final stages of Castlereagh's illness were directed at two individuals, his widow and his doctor. Lord Liverpool, the Prime Minister, was inclined to blame the widow, and he told Princess Lieven as much shortly after the funeral.

'Yesterday,' wrote the Princess to Metternich on 23rd August 1822, 'Lord Liverpool gave me the most plausible explanation of the way Lord Londonderry was neglected. His wife had known the state he was in for a long time; but her pride was stronger than her anxiety. She would not confide such a secret to anybody in the world. When, at last, the King's interview with Londonderry, and, afterwards, the Duke of Wellington made the truth clear, she continued to treat it as unimportant, in order that the journey on the Continent might not be cancelled. According to Lord Liverpool, Lady Londonderry had the journey very much at heart. She wanted it at all costs, and, the day before the tragedy, she wrote to Liverpool that her husband was very well and that nothing would prevent his leaving on the 15th for the Continent. It was to her advantage, then, to remove him from the observation of other people; that was why none of his intimate friends even saw him during his last days, and why she opposed with all her might the idea of the doctor calling in a colleague. As to the treatment of his patient, the doctor seems to have nothing to blame himself for.'

This account is not altogether accurate. It is true that Emily Lady Londonderry did write to the Prime Minister —on 10th August, as we have seen—but, far from seeking to disguise her husband's condition, she stated that he had been 'very unwell for some days'. At the same time, there is no doubt that she was most eager to accompany her husband to the Continent, particularly since she had been very disappointed at having to remain at home when Castlereagh went to Hanover with the King in the previous year; and it is clear that she hoped that, with a few days' rest and careful nursing, he might be able to leave on the date which had been fixed for their setting out together. As for Princess Lieven's statement that Emily opposed the calling in of a second doctor, it may or may not be true. There is no discovered evidence of corroboration on this point.

On the other hand, there is also no doubt that Dr. Bankhead was generally blamed for failing in his duty as a physician towards his patient. There was even some talk at the time that he might be indicted on a charge of manslaughter, but nothing came of this. It is doubtful if proceedings of this kind were seriously considered by the authorities, although Brougham suggested that they should be taken. Since his coming to London from the north of Ireland, Dr. Bankhead had, thanks largely to Castlereagh's patronage, succeeded in building up what is commonly called a society practice, in spite of current rumours that he sometimes took advantage of his female patients to the extent that 'maids, wives and widows were often obliged to pull their bells for protection'. His patients now deserted him and he was soon reduced to severe financial straits. He seems to have been too proud to beg for charity, and there exists a pathetic letter, dated 4th December 1823, which he wrote to Emily, returning a sum of money she had sent him, but asking her at the same time if she would use her good offices with the Government to secure him a pension so that he 'might yet be rescued from beggary'.

'For the last year and more,' he wrote, 'in consequence of much misrepresentation (and chiefly among families of rank), my professional profits have almost wholly fallen off.' He went on to say that he had stated personally to Lord Liverpool, and also more than once to the Duke of Wellington, 'as they both knew every circumstance', the difficulties in which he was placed. They both, according to Bankhead, particularly the Duke, expressed the opinion that 'as they felt I had acted *correctly as a Physician*, I had a just claim upon the Government in consequence of injury sustained by a public calamity'. The Duke at a more recent interview added that a word in support from his late patient's widow would carry additional weight.

No doubt Emily Lady Londonderry, who seems to have stuck to the unfortunate doctor all along, did as he requested. What effect it had on the authorities is not known. But it is doubtful if anything was done for him. What does appear, however, is that he was able to leave London and settle in Florence, where he was reported many years later as having died at the age of ninety-one. This was probably made possible by his son, who held various posts in the diplomatic service including Minister in Mexico City and Washington.

But this is not the whole story of Dr. Bankhead. According to Mrs. Arbuthnot, 'that beast', as she called him, 'since he has found himself blamed by the world for his neglect of Lord Londonderry in his illness, has gone about saying he was not mad but that his death was a mystery known only to himself and Lord Liverpool!' It further appears from the same source that Bankhead later became more explicit. It was common knowledge that Castlereagh had accused himself of having committed a homosexual offence, since the King had repeated to a fairly wide circle of acquaintances what had passed at their last interview. Bankhead, it appears, now asserted that he had actually received a confession of guilt from his patient; or, as Mrs. Arbuthnot put it, 'when Bankhead found that the whole world abused him for his neglect of Lord Londonderry, he immediately determined to endeavour to justify himself by saying that Lord Londonderry was not mad, and that the crime of which he accused himself he had actually committed'. He subsequently confided as much to Wellington, who was at first inclined to believe what he had heard but later revised his opinion.

'He came to the Duke,' noted Mrs. Arbuthnot, who obtained these particulars from her friend, 'and told him a long story of what Lord Londonderry had himself told him and stated to him *two facts* and told it all so plausibly that he actually made the Duke believe there was some truth in what he said. However, luckily, the Duke ascertained *beyond a doubt* that *the facts were both positively false*; and he told me that he had not a shadow of doubt of the falsehood of all Bankhead's story, which he says he is perfectly certain was made up for his own purpose; and that, finding how much he was abused, he had the baseness to seize upon the delusion of a mind broke down with the pressure of business to sully the character of the noblest, most high-minded creature that ever existed, for the purpose of saving his own miserable credit.'

Mrs. Arbuthnot comments that the matter was 'too atrocious to dwell upon' and she does not reveal what the facts were which Wellington mentioned. On the other hand, Emily seems to have attached some credence to the story, as she was in correspondence some months later with Wellington on the subject. However, the Duke would have none of it. 'I have reflected maturely upon what you told me yesterday,' he wrote to her on 3rd March 1824, 'and considering the period at which he gave you the information, the unfortunate malady under which there can be no doubt that he laboured for some time, and my own conviction from what I have long seen and observed, I cannot but think that you have been misinformed, and that you ought to attribute what he told you to one of the unfortunate delusions of the moment.'

For about eighteen months after her husband's death Emily Lady Londonderry lived quietly at Cray nursing her grief and saw few people. Then she suddenly determined to come out in society again. Lord George Seymour, the father of Castlereagh's private secretary, Hamilton Seymour, was at Cray towards the end of 1823 and wrote to Lord Liverpool: 'I am sure you will be glad to hear that I found Lady Londonderry wonderfully mended. She has determined to go to town in January, which I think very judicious; in short, the more she can face the old habits, the sooner the better with propriety.'

This view was not shared by, among others, Mrs. Arbuthnot, who took umbrage that Emily persistently cut her and her husband at parties. 'The King,' she wrote on 17th March 1824, 'has given us a fine print of Lord Londonderry from a picture by Lawrence in his robes of the Garter. It is wonderfully like. Lady Londonderry has come out again into the world as gay as ever and appearing to have forgot that such a man ever lived. I always thought her generally an unfeeling woman, but I had thought all the affections of her nature were devoted to him and certainly was not prepared for such total want of almost decency.'

Not long afterwards Emily was reported to be in failing health. She died in St. James's Square on 12th February 1829. Eight days later, on her fifty-seventh birthday, she was buried beside her husband in Westminster Abbey.

6

We now come to the core of the story. Granted that Castlereagh believed during his last days that he was about to be publicly denounced as a homosexual—he said as much to the King, to Mrs. Arbuthnot and to other close friends— the question may naturally be asked: are there any grounds for supposing that he had in fact committed a homosexual offence, as indeed his physician later apparently suggested? If not, what possible explanation can be advanced for the delusion under which he was obviously labouring?

The answer to the first question is no. There are no such grounds. As for the second, there is a perfectly feasible explanation, which has long been known, and which the present writer is convinced is the correct one. It has received strong corroboration from the recently published letters and journals of Princess Lieven and Mrs. Arbuthnot, who were not merely contemporary witnesses but also close personal friends of Lord Castlereagh. It is also consistent with the evidence given at the Coroner's inquest. However commentators, at least in recent times, while indicating the substance of the explanation, have been unwilling to refer to the details in print. The first writer in the present century to allude to it was Sir Herbert Maxwell, first in his life of Wellington, published in 1900, and then in his edition of *The Creevey Papers*, which appeared in 1903. 'And now for Castlereagh—what an extraordinary event!' Mr. Creevey had written two days after the tragedy. 'I take for granted his self-destruction has been one of the common cases of pressure upon the brain which produces irritability, ending in derangement.' Creevey also referred to the charge made against him by Napoleon, as related to his surgeon Dr. Barry O'Mearn, that Castlereagh had misappropriated some money which was rightfully his and this 'has had something to do with it'. Maxwell dismissed these causes as wide of the mark and then proceeded to give what he considered the true one. 'Castlereagh had submitted to a peculiarly nefarious system of blackmail by some villains who had entrapped him, and the agony of apprehension resulting from this, acting upon a mind perhaps overstrained in the public service during a long and peculiarly agitated period, brought about the disaster.'

Maxwell gave no further particulars. Six years later he was followed in scarcely more explicit terms by William Toynbee,* in his book *Glimpses of the Twenties*, in which a chapter is devoted to Castlereagh's career. 'That he had actually been culpable, and not merely the victim of a cruel stroke of misfortune, it is difficult to believe,' wrote Toynbee. 'There were not wanting among his contemporaries who hinted at the former view; but be it at once said they were avowed political enemies, whose cherished object was to encompass his ruin. It is, therefore, only fair to adopt the version which receives credence to this day from the great Party to which he belonged, namely, that he had been deliberately entrapped into a gravely equivocal position in

*Eldest son of Joseph Toynbee, the aural surgeon, and brother of Arnold Toynbee the social philosopher and economist.

order to be made the object of systematic extortion, and that, taken by surprise, he lacked the requisite firmness to resist and expose his persecutors.'

Exactly how Castlereagh came to be blackmailed, the details of which neither Maxwell nor Toynbee felt justified in divulging when they wrote, is as follows.

When Parliament was sitting and the weather was fine, the Minister was in the habit of walking home from the House to St. James's Square. From time to time he was accosted by women of the streets, and to the importunities of some of them he was, unfortunately for him, induced more than once to listen. Whether he thought he could indulge himself in this manner and remain undetected for long is not known. The fact remains that his identity was soon discovered, among others apparently by a man named Jennings, as we have already seen, and also by seven scoundrels who had observed his behaviour on these nocturnal walks, and they laid an ingenious trap for him. It is not clear whether Jennings and the others were in collusion; in all probability they acted separately and independently of each other.

As a result of a casual encounter one night during the session of 1819, Castlereagh was taken by his companion to a certain house, where they were both shown into an apartment furnished in the conventional manner of a brothel. His companion began to undress, when to his horrified amazement Castlereagh discovered that the person who had brought him here was not a woman, as he had supposed, but a youth dressed in woman's clothes and disguised to pass as a woman. What happened then may best be described in the words of the only existing account of the incident.

He had no time for reflection or delay as to what course to take, the door of the room was forced open, a couple

153

of villains rushed in and accused him of being about to commit an act from which nature shrinks with horror; adding at the same time that they knew perfectly well who he was. The purport of the accusation was palpable, and unfortunately, in the intensity of the crisis, the Marquess lost his presence of mind and his courage. He adopted the course which they suggested, and gave them all the money he had about him to secure his immediate escape. This course was precisely what they had plotted to bring about. They had secured their victim, he was in their power, and they were resolved to let him know that their silence could only be obtained by full compliance with their extortionate demands.

Day after day did these miscreants station themselves by the iron railings with which the enclosure of St. James's Square is surrounded, opposite the windows of the residence of the Marquess, and take the opportunity, by signs and motions whenever he appeared, to let him know that they had not yet forgotten the scene which they had contrived. Driven almost to distraction by this persecution, he made known his case, with all the circumstances, to the late Duke of Wellington and to another nobleman. By them he was advised to give the wretches into custody at once, avow the full facts, and extricate himself from further disgusting thraldom.

He had not the resolution to follow this advice. He shrank from the consequences which the painful disclosure of what was really to be deplored in his conduct might produce on the feelings of his wife; and in a moment of distraction adopted the desperate remedy which was to extricate him from his persecutors and himself.

The foregoing account appears in a work entitled *Recollections of the Last Half Century*, by the Rev. J. Richardson, which was privately printed for the author in London in 1855. According to Mr. Richardson, he obtained the story from a reliable informant, who had in turn received it from 'the mouth of a noble lord still living, with whom the Marquess was on terms of social intimacy, and with whom he was connected by political ties'. The primary source of information would appear to be identical with the other nobleman, to whom, on the authority of Mr. Richardson's narrative, Castlereagh revealed some part at least of the blackmailing story, besides the Duke of Wellington. There can be little if any doubt that this was Lord Clanwilliam, the Parliamentary Under-Secretary for Foreign Affairs and an intimate personal friend of Castlereagh, whose private secretary he had previously been. He was the only member of the dead statesman's small and intimate circle who was alive in 1855.

At the time of the tragedy at Cray, Clanwilliam was a young man of twenty-seven, who had only recently been confirmed in his Foreign Office post. He was the first person apart from the family relatives whom the widowed Emily would consent to see on the fatal 12th August, as it was he who, at her request, made arrangements for the funeral in Westminster Abbey. To Clanwilliam was also entrusted the painful task of breaking the news to Castlereagh's brother Charles Stewart, the Ambassador in Vienna, which he did in a long letter he wrote on the same day and finished after the Coroner's inquest had taken place. (Incidentally, the letter was intercepted by Metternich's secret police and a copy was made before it reached the Ambassador.) This letter ended on a peculiar note, which cannot be dismissed as devoid of significance, since it is evidence that Clanwilliam knew something of what was going on at the back of his late chief's mind. 'There is but one subject on which there remains anything to say,' wrote Clanwilliam, 'and that is the matters on which his head turned during the different moments of delirium. This I will reserve for future conversation when we meet.'

The account given by Mr. Richardson is corroborated by the statements which Mrs. Arbuthnot and Princess Lieven recorded at the time in private and confidential form. Writing in her journal on 28th August 1822—just over a fortnight after Castlereagh's death—Mrs. Arbuthnot remarked that on the Monday (5th August) when Castlereagh called on her, he admitted, after having carefully questioned her as to whether she had heard anything against him, that 'about three years before he had had an anonymous letter threatening to tell of his having been seen going into an inproper house.' It may be remembered that Mrs. Arbuthnot twitted the Minister on this occasion to the effect that she had often heard he was a great flirt and very fond of the ladies. (Incidentally, this reputation is borne out by the famous Regency courtesan Harriet Wilson, who has recalled in her memoirs that Castlereagh flattered her vanity by merely looking at her. 'He certainly looked a great deal more than perhaps his lady might have thought civil,' she added with a characteristic touch of feminine malice.) Mrs. Arbuthnot's account continues: 'It appears that three years ago he did go with a woman to an improper house from which he was watched by a man, who the next morning wrote to tell him so and asked for a place. However, at that time he thought not of it.' It was only much later, according to Mrs. Arbuthnot, that 'so strongly had business and fatigue upset his mind that he actually fancied the purport of the letter was to accuse him of a crime not to be named, and this notion could not be put out of his head'.

The anonymous letter here referred to was probably written by the man Jennings. Mrs. Arbuthnot conveys the impression that Castlereagh thought that the same letter contained the more serious accusation as well, but it seems that this was actually contained in a second anonymous letter. On this point Princess Lieven is quite explicit. Writing to Metternich two days after Castlereagh's death, she positively states that at his last visit to Carlton House he produced two letters. 'He showed the King two anonymous letters,' she wrote on 14th August. 'One of them threatened to reveal his irregular conduct to his wife; the other concerned a more terrible subject. This second letter sent him off his head.'

Richardson's explanation is further corroborated by the evidence of the inquest, where it was made abundantly clear by the two witnesses that in his last days and hours Castlereagh was obsessed with the idea that he was the victim of a conspiracy. In particular, it will be remembered, Mrs. Robinson, the maid, stated that during the previous fortnight 'he repeatedly said some persons had conspired against him'. In view of this testimony, it is remarkable that the Coroner did not pursue this aspect of the tragedy further and ask the witness 'Did he say who the persons were?' Such a question as this might well have elicited information which would have put the case in a clearer light.

What Mrs. Robinson did say, however, was that, whenever he saw two people speaking together, such as his wife and the doctor, he always said, 'There is a conspiracy laid against me.' In this she was supported by Dr. Bankhead, who referred to his patient's expression of suspicion and alarm at his abrupt questioning as to whether the doctor had anything unpleasant to tell him. Thus it seems clear, from the testimony of these witnesses, that though Castlereagh's mind was under a delusion as to the actual persons mentioned in evidence as being the conspirators against him, the delusion was produced by the unfortunate existence of a real conspiracy which had turned his brain, and that to a certain extent there was a meaning in his madness, incomprehensible to the witnesses, but which was nevertheless acting powerfully on his mind and driving him towards suicide.

The final word may be left with Philip von Neumann, the Counsellor at the Austrian Embassy in London, who was greatly puzzled by what had happened. 'The more one knew of Lord Londonderry,' he wrote on the day of the tragedy, 'the less can one understand what could have led him to commit such an act. Of all men he was the last from whom one would have expected anything of the kind. There is some mystery about this which perhaps Time will explain; but whatever it was, it must have been something very serious to have led to such an act.'